Eyes Open 2
Student's Book

Ben Goldstein & Ceri Jones
with **Emma Heyderman**

Starter Unit	Vocabulary		Language focus	
	p4 Family **p5** School subjects **p6** Sports and activities		**p4** *be*, subject pronouns, possessive *'s*, **p5** *there is/are*, *some* and *any*, *have got* + *a/an*, **p7** Present simple affirmative, negative and questions, adverbs of frequency	

Unit	Vocabulary	Reading	Language focus 1	Listening and vocabulary
1 **Money matters**	**p9** Shops	**p10** A blog **Explore** extreme adjectives	**p11** Present simple vs. continuous **Get it right!** *-ing* ▶ Unusual fun	**p12** A radio programme Money verbs
2 **Our heroes**	**p19** Jobs	**p20** A magazine quiz **Explore** expressions with *make*	**p21** *was/were*: affirmative and negative Past simple and time expressions ▶ Wildlife hero **Say it right!** Irregular past verbs p96	**p22** A conversation Adjectives of character
	Review Unit 1 and 2 page 28–29			
3 **Strange stories**	**p31** Action verbs	**p32** A newspaper article **Explore** expressions with *look*	**p33** Past continuous ▶ Mystery in the mountains	**p34** A strange story Adverbs of manner **Get it right!** Irregular adverbs
4 **At home**	**p41** Things in the home	**p42** An online forum **Explore** expressions with *do*	**p43** Comparatives and superlatives ▶ Moving house **Say it right!** *schwa* p96	**p44** An interview Household appliances
	Review Unit 3 and 4 page 50–51			
5 **Visions of the future**	**p53** Computer words	**p54** A magazine article **Explore** suffixes *-ful* and *-less*	**p55** *will/won't* *may/might* **Get it right!** *will/won't* + infinitive without *to* ▶ Pizza problems **Say it right!** *won't/want* p96	**p56** An interview Technology verbs + prepositions
6 **Life choices**	**p63** Life events	**p64** A magazine quiz **Explore** phrasal verbs 2	**p65** *will* vs. *be going to* **Get it right!** *will* for instant decisions ▶ A school at home **Say it right!** Contractions: *will* p97	**p66** A conversation Containers and materials
	Review Unit 5 and 6 page 72–73			
7 **Look out!**	**p75** Accidents and injuries	**p76** A magazine article **Explore** expressions with *get*	**p77** Present perfect: affirmative and negative **Get it right!** *been* and *gone* ▶ Danger in our food	**p78** A radio interview The body
8 **Having fun!**	**p85** Free time activities	**p86** An online forum **Explore** expressions with *have*	**p87** *one/ones* Indefinite pronouns **Get it right!** *any* + negative verbs ▶ A New York City food tour	**p88** A radio interview Adjectives of feeling **Say it right!** Word stress in adjectives of feeling p97
	Review Unit 7 and 8 page 94–95			

Projects p124–126　　Irregular verbs and phonemic script p127

Speaking and listening

p4 Nathan's family
p5 Nathan's school
p6 Nathan's free time

Language focus 2	Discover Culture (Video and Reading)	Speaking	Writing	Extras
p13 want to, would like, would prefer to and enough + noun **Get it right!** would like **Say it right!** enough /f/ p96	**p14** ▶ Tiger sanctuary **p15** An article **Explore** adjective prefixes	**p16** ▶ **Real talk:** How do you spend your money? Functions for shopping	**p17** An email **Useful language:** Imperatives	**p116 CLIL** Maths – percentages ▶ What does Zero mean? **p100** Grammar reference **p108** Vocabulary bank
p23 was/were questions Past simple questions **Get it right!** did + infinitive	**p24** ▶ The Chilean Mine Rescue **p25** A blog **Explore** the suffix -ness	**p26** ▶ **Real talk:** Who's your role model and why? Speculating	**p27** A description of a person you admire **Useful language:** Connectors	**p117 CLIL** History – The feudal system ▶ Amelia Earhart, famous flyer **p101** Grammar reference **p109** Vocabulary bank
p35 Past simple vs. continuous could(n't)	**p36** ▶ A story from under the sea **p37** An article **Explore** nouns with -er	**p38** ▶ **Real talk:** What's an unusual or interesting thing that happened to you recently? Telling someone your news	**p39** A story **Useful language:** Sequencing language 1	**p118 CLIL** Art – Making a comic ▶ Behind the scenes **p102** Grammar reference **p110** Vocabulary bank
p45 must/mustn't and should/shouldn't **Get it right!** Modals + bare infinitive	**p46** ▶ A cool life **p47** A blog **Explore** verbs with up or down	**p48** ▶ **Real talk:** Which do you prefer – flats or houses? Asking for and offering help	**p49** A description of a house **Useful language:** Order of adjectives	**p119 CLIL** Art – The Bauhaus movement ▶ The seventh wonder of the world **p103** Grammar reference **p111** Vocabulary bank
p57 First conditional	**p58** ▶ Learning to share **p59** A blog **Explore** phrasal verbs 1	**p60** ▶ **Real talk:** How important is your mobile to you? Asking for and giving instructions	**p61** An opinion essay **Useful language:** Sequencing language 2	**p120 CLIL** ICT – Supercomputers ▶ Who's real? **p104** Grammar reference **p112** Vocabulary bank
p67 Present continuous for future	**p68** ▶ Time for an adventure! **p69** A magazine article **Explore** verbs with prepositions	**p70** ▶ **Real talk:** What are you going to do when you leave school? Agreeing and disagreeing	**p71** A thank you email **Useful language:** Verb patterns	**p121 CLIL** Science – Lifecycle of a plastic bag ▶ Go green! **p105** Grammar reference **p113** Vocabulary bank
p79 Present perfect questions Past simple vs. present perfect **Say it right!** Present perfect or past simple p97	**p80** ▶ A deadly job **p81** An article **Explore** compound nouns	**p82** ▶ **Real talk:** Have you ever had an accident? Reacting to news	**p83** An email refusing an invitation **Useful language:** Polite language for refusing	**p122 CLIL** Science – Foodborne illness ▶ Medical myths **p106** Grammar reference **p114** Vocabulary bank
p89 too + adjective (+ infinitive), (not) adjective + enough **Get it right!** too or enough	**p90** ▶ Punkin Chunkin! **p91** An article **Explore** making nouns from verbs	**p92** ▶ **Real talk:** How do you celebrate your birthday? Making and responding to suggestions	**p93** An email invitation to a friend **Useful language:** Referencing words	**p123 CLIL** Geography – Functional Zones ▶ An ancient answer **p107** Grammar reference **p115** Vocabulary bank

Starter Unit

Family

1 🔊 **1.01** Listen and complete Nathan's family tree with the names in the box.

Sophie   Dave   Ben   Henry   Anne
Tom   Phil   Diana   Marie   Lucy

2 Complete the table with the words in the box.

~~parents~~   ~~mum~~   ~~brother~~   husband   dad
aunt   sister   grandma   cousin   uncle
wife   granddad   grandparents

mum,   brother,   parents,

Subject pronouns and *be*

3 Complete the examples from the listening in Exercise 1.

	I	you / we / they	he / she / it
+	I ¹ *'m* Nathan.	You're 13.	He ² …. from Newcastle.
–	I'm not Matthew.	You aren't 12.	My dad ³ …. from Liverpool.
?	Am I right?	Are you from Scotland?	⁴ …. your family big?

➡ Grammar reference • page 98

4 Complete the questions with the correct form of *be*. Then complete the answers with the correct subject pronoun.

1. Where *'s* your mum from?
   She 's from Barcelona.
2. What …. your dad's name? ….'s Pete.
3. …. you in a sports team?
   Yes, …. am. ….'m in the basketball team.
4. How old …. your granddad? ….'s 82.
5. …. your parents teachers? No, …. aren't.

Possessive *'s*

5 Look at the examples from the listening in Exercise 1 and put the apostrophe (') in the correct place.

1. My mums name is Marie.
2. My grandparents names are Henry and Diana.

➡ Grammar reference • page 98

Your turn

6 Write questions with the correct form of *be* and possessive *'s*. Use one word from each box. Then ask and answer the questions with your partner.

Where	parents	favourite singer
What	classmates	favourite book
Who	cousin	birthday
When	best friend	English lesson

When's your mum's birthday?

It's on 20 May.

4

School subjects

1 Complete the school subjects. Then match them with the pictures.

1. Fr _ nch
2. _ ngl _ sh
3. M _ s _ c
4. Sc _ enc _
5. _ CT
6. P _
7. G _ _ gr _ phy
8. M _ ths
9. H _ st _ ry

2 🔊 **1.02** Listen to Nathan talking to his cousin Lucy about his school. Which of the school subjects in Exercise 1 do you hear?

there is/are and some and any

3 Complete the examples from the listening in Exercise 2. When do we use *some* and *any*?

	Singular	Plural
+	There ¹.... **some** cola in the fridge.	There ³.... **some** classrooms in the main building.
–	There **isn't any** orange juice.	There ⁴.... **any** laptops in our classroom.
?	².... **there any** orange juice?	⁵.... **there any** science labs at your school?

➡ Grammar reference • page 98

4 Write sentences with *there is/are* and *some/any* about the things and places in your school in the box below.

> <s>posters</s> food computers balls laptops
> students science lab <s>classroom walls</s>
> library IT room canteen sports hall

There are some posters on the classroom walls.

have got + a/an

5 Complete the examples from the listening in Exercise 2.

	I / you / we / they	he / she / it
+	I ¹.... PE tomorrow.	My school's ⁴.... four labs.
–	We ².... **got an** IT room.	It **hasn't got** any laptops.
?	**Have** you ³.... a big sports hall?	**Has** Lucy **got** a laptop?

➡ Grammar reference • page 99

Your turn

6 Write questions with *have got*. Use the people and the things below. Then ask and answer your questions with a partner.

> you
> your best friend
> your mum, etc.
> your teacher
> your classmates

> Maths, History, PE, etc.
> a big family
> a mountain bike
> a laptop
> an English dictionary

Have you got PE today?   *Yes, I have.*

Sports and activities

1 Match the pictures with the sports in the box.

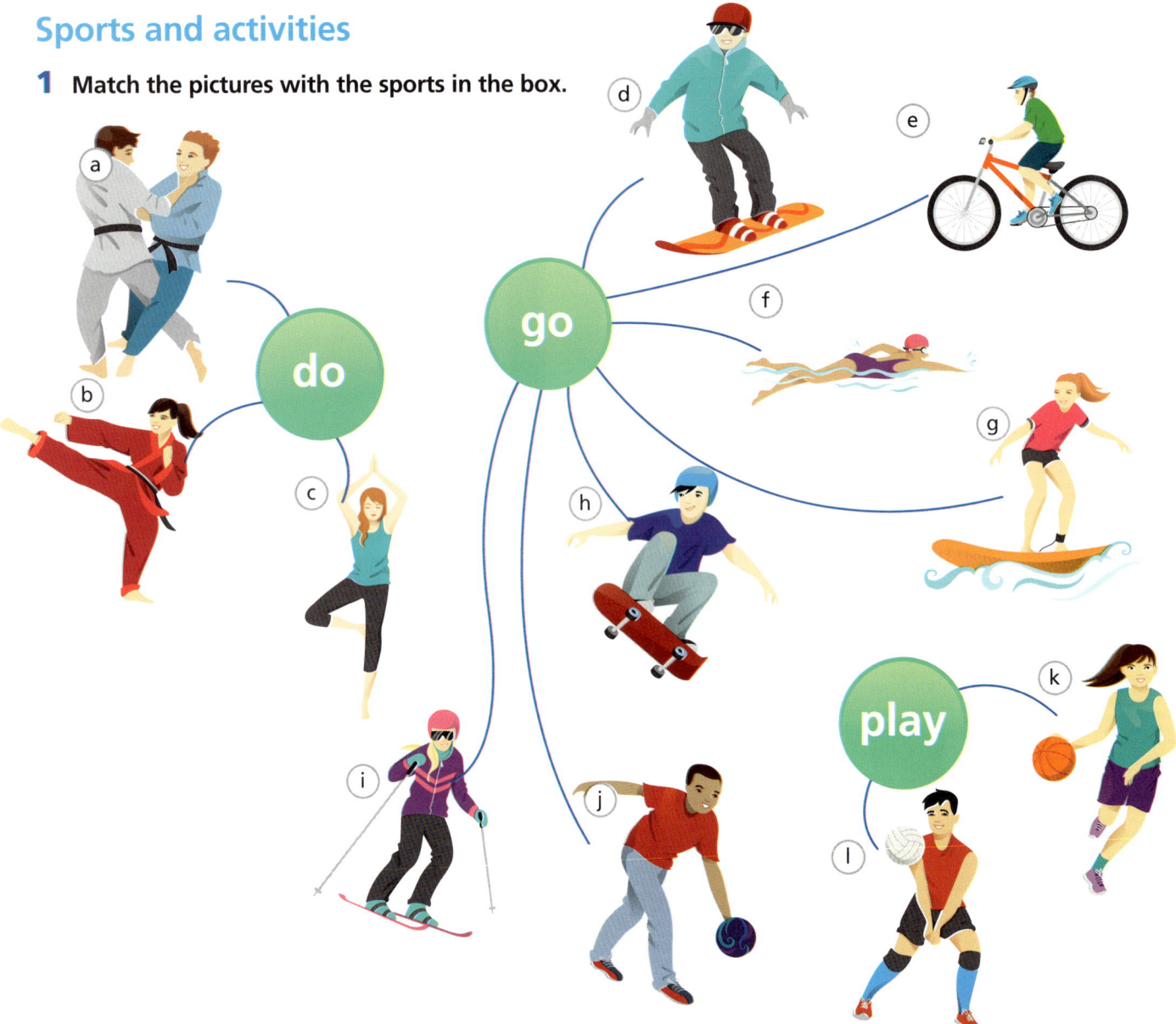

judo   volleyball   bowling   skiing   swimming
snowboarding   cycling   skateboarding
basketball   surfing   karate   yoga

2 🔊 **1.03** Listen to Nathan and Lucy talking about their free time. Which of the sports and activities in Exercise 1 does Nathan do? Which of them does Lucy do?

Present simple: affirmative and negative

3 Complete the examples from the listening in Exercise 2.

	I / you / we / they	he / she / it
+	I ¹ _like_ surfing My friends and I usually ³ .... cycling.	He sometimes ² .... bowling with granddad.
−	You **don't** ⁴ .... near the sea.	He ⁵ .... **like** it very much.

➡ **Grammar reference • page 99**

4 Complete the sentences with the present simple form of the verb in brackets.
1 I .... (go) snowboarding with my parents in the winter.
2 My friends .... (have) football training on Fridays.
3 I .... (not play) volleyball very often.
4 My sister .... (do) drama after school.
5 My uncle .... (not play) chess.
6 My friends and I .... (ride) our bikes to school every day.
7 We .... (not live) near the sea so I .... (not go) surfing.

5 Rewrite the sentences in Exercise 4 so they are true for you.
1 *I don't go snowboarding with my parents in the winter. We don't live near the mountains.*

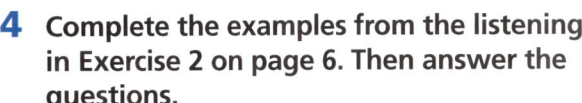

Present simple: questions

1 Complete the examples from the listening on page 6.

	I / you / we / they	he / she / it
Wh-?	What sports ¹*do* you **do**? When **do** they **go** bowling?	How often **does** he **go** snowboarding?
Y/N?	² .... you **go** swimming?	³ .... your sister **go** surfing too?
Short answers	Yes, I **do**. No, I ⁴	Yes, she ⁵ .... No, he **doesn't**.

➜ Grammar reference • page 99

2 Write questions about your sentences in Exercise 5 on page 6.
1. When / you / go snowboarding?
   When do you go snowboarding?
2. When / your friends / have training?
3. you / play volleyball?
4. your sister / do drama after school?
5. What sports and activities / your uncle / do?
6. How / you and your friends / go to school?
7. you / go surfing?

Your turn

3 Work with a partner. Ask and answer your questions in Exercise 2.

> When do you go snowboarding?

> I don't go snowboarding with my parents in the winter. We don't live near the mountains. What about you?

Adverbs of frequency

4 Complete the examples from the listening in Exercise 2 on page 6. Then answer the questions.
1. My friends and I .... go cycling on Saturday afternoons.
2. I .... go swimming with Mum and Dad.
3. The water's .... cold.
4. He .... goes now.

> 1 Does the abverb of frequency go before or after the verb *be*?
> 2 Does the adverb of frequency go before or after other verbs?

➜ Grammar reference • page 99

5 Rewrite the sentences with the adverbs of frequency in the correct place.
1. We do ICT in the IT room. (usually)
   We usually do ICT in the IT room.
2. My friends play basketball at school. (sometimes)
3. I do yoga at school. (never)
4. My grandparents go bowling. (sometimes)
5. My cousin does judo at the weekend. (often)
6. I go cycling on Sunday morning. (always)

Your turn

6 Write true sentences about you. Use the present simple, adverbs of frequency and the words below.
- have lunch in the school canteen
- be tired on Monday morning
- play basketball in the sports hall
- go bowling
- go swimming in the sea
- do Science in the science lab

I always have lunch in the school canteen.

7 Work with a partner. Use 'How often…?' and the present simple to ask and answer questions about your sentences in Exercise 6.

> How often do you have lunch in the school canteen?

> I always have lunch in the school canteen.

1 Money matters

Discovery EDUCATION

In this unit ...

Unusual fun p11

Tiger sanctuary p14

Shopping p16

CLIL What does Zero mean? p116

Vocabulary
- Shops
- Money verbs
- Extreme adjectives
- Adjective prefixes

Language focus
- Present continuous
- Present simple vs. continuous
- *would prefer to, would(n't) like to, don't want to*
- *enough*

Unit aims
I can ...
- talk about shops and shopping centres.
- talk about the things I'm doing now and the things I do every day.
- understand a conversation about how young people spend their money.
- describe things I want to, would like to or would prefer to do.
- understand information about charities.
- ask for things in shops.
- write an email asking for advice.

BE CURIOUS

What can you see in the photo?
Start thinking
- What can you buy at this market?
- Where do you think it is?
- Where do you buy things in your town?

Vocabulary Shops

1 🔊 1.04 Match the pictures with the words in the box. Then listen, check and repeat.

> bookshop   chemist   clothes shop
> department store   electronics shop
> music shop   newsagent   shoe shop
> sports shop   supermarket

2 Look at Exercise 1.
Which places sell …
1 food and drink?
2 things to read?
3 things to wear?

Where can you …
4 buy a new computer?
5 listen to music?
6 go when you feel ill?

Your turn

3 Write your answers to the questions.
1 What kind of shops do you like?
2 When do you go there?
3 Who do you go with?
4 What do you buy there?

My favourite shop is a music shop. I go there on Saturday with my friends.

4 Work with a partner. Ask and answer the questions in Exercise 3.

➡ **Vocabulary bank** • page 108

Reading A blog

1 Look at the photos of a shopping centre in Dubai. What can you do there?

2 🔊 **1.05** Read Liam's blog and check your ideas to Exercise 1. Then match the photos to the places in bold.
   a *Sega Republic*

3 Read Liam's blog again. What are the numbers about?

   1200   22   120   50 million   150

🔍 **Explore** extreme adjectives

4 Look at the adjectives from Liam's blog. Do they mean *very good* or *very bad*?

   great   awful   wonderful
   brilliant   amazing

5 Find three adjectives in the text that mean *very hot*, *very cold* and *very big*. Do we use *very* or *absolutely* before these adjectives?

   ➡ Vocabulary bank • page 108

🗨 **Your turn**

6 Work with a partner. Ask and answer the questions.
   1 Would you like to visit the Dubai Mall?
   2 What would you like to do there?
   3 Are there many shopping centres in your town?
   4 How often do you go there?
   5 What other things can you do there?

HOME   < OLDER POSTS   SUBSCRIBE

AN ENGLISH BOY IN DUBAI

I'm Liam. I'm 15 years old and I'm from Cambridge. My parents are working in Dubai this year so I'm writing all my news about life here on this blog. Hope you like it!

A DAY AT THE MALL
POSTED BY ENGLISHBOYINDUBAI
🕐 SATURDAY 20 APRIL

Today I'm spending the day in Dubai Mall with my family. It's great! It's got about 1,200 shops, 22 cinema screens and 120 cafés and restaurants.

More than 50 million people visit the mall every year because there are a lot of cool things to do here. Luckily, there aren't only shops because I hate shopping. It's awful! My dad and my sister are watching the fish right now in the wonderful **Underwater Zoo**. There are more than 33,000 fish there – even sharks!

Outside it's boiling so why am I wearing a sweater? Because I'm skating on the **Olympic-size ice rink** and it's absolutely freezing. The temperature of the ice is below zero! After the ice rink, I want to go to the mall's theme park, the **Sega Republic**. It's brilliant – it's got 150 games and rides.

And what are my mum and aunt doing? They're looking at the **Dancing Fountain**. It's 152 metres high! At night, there's an amazing light show. On a clear night, you can see it from space!

a

b

c

FACT! The Dubai Mall is absolutely huge! It's the size of 50 football pitches. It's the biggest shopping centre in the world!

d

Language focus 1 Present continuous

1 Complete the examples from the text on page 10.

I	he / she / it	you / we / they
+	I ¹.... **spending** the day in Dubai Mall.	My friend **is shopping**.	My dad and my sister **are** ².... the fish.
–	I'**m not going** to the zoo.	Liam's mum **isn't shopping**.	Liam's dad and sister **aren't skating**.
?	Why ³.... I **wearing** a sweater?	**Is** Liam **wearing** a sweater?	What **are** my mum and aunt ⁴.... ?

➔ Grammar reference • page 100

👁 Get it right!
Spelling the *-ing* form:
For verbs ending in -e, remove the e: *write* → *writing*
For verbs ending with one vowel and one consonant, double the final consonant: *shop* → *shopping*

2 Write sentences in the present continuous with the verbs in brackets.
1. They .... (write) text messages on their phones.
   They're writing text messages on their phones.
2. He .... (not listen) to the teacher!
3. I .... (make) a cake for my brother's birthday.
4. We .... (not watch) TV. There's nothing to watch!
5. Nicky .... (run) in the park today.

3 Write questions in the present continuous. Then answer them for you.
1. What / your teacher / do?
   What is your teacher doing? She's writing on the board.
2. Where / you / sit / now?
3. Why / you / learn English?
4. you / listen to music / at the moment?
5. your friends / play football / now?

Present simple vs. continuous

4 Read the sentences from Liam's blog and answer the questions. Then complete the rule with *simple* or *continuous*.
   a. Today **I'm spending** the day in Dubai Mall.
   b. More than 50 million people **visit** the mall every year.
1. Which sentence talks about an action in progress?
2. Which sentence talks about a fact, habit or routine?

We use the **present** ³.... to talk about facts, habits and routines and the **present** ⁴.... to talk about an action in progress.

➔ Grammar reference • page 100

Your turn

5 Complete the questions with the present simple or present continuous form of the verb in brackets.
1. What .... you .... (do) now?
2. What do you think your parents .... (do) now?
3. What .... you usually .... (do) at the weekend?
4. Where .... you usually .... (go) after school?
5. What .... your classmates .... (do) now?
6. Where .... you usually .... (go) on holiday?
7. .... you .... (read) a good book at the moment?

6 Work with a partner. Ask and answer the questions in Exercise 5.

> What are you doing now?

> I'm talking to you in my English class!

Learn about having fun in Dubai.
- Where are the young people snowboarding outdoors?
- Where are they snowboarding indoors?
- What shop do the young people like visiting?

1.1 Unusual fun

Listening A radio programme

1 Look at the photos. Which things have you got?

2 🔊 1.06 Listen to a radio programme. Which of the things in Exercise 1 have Josh and Megan got in their bags?

3 🔊 1.06 Listen again and choose the correct answers.
1. Josh wants to buy **a games console / a mobile phone**.
2. Josh is shopping with **his pocket money / his birthday money**.
3. Josh and his family **buy / don't buy** clothes online.
4. Josh is shopping with **his family / his friends**.
5. Megan **gets / doesn't get** pocket money.
6. Megan **likes / doesn't like** getting money for her birthday.

sunglasses    cap    games console

T-shirt    football

tablet    trainers

Vocabulary Money verbs

4 🔊 1.07 Look at the pictures and complete the sentences with the present continuous form of the verbs in the box. Then listen, check and repeat.

> earn   sell   borrow   buy   save   spend

1 He …. his bike.

4 He …. all his money on some new trainers.

2 He …. money in a jar.

5 He …. money washing his dad's car.

3 He …. a book.

6 He …. money from his brother.

5 Choose the correct words.
1. I never **sell / buy / borrow** clothes online. I like to try them on first.
2. I don't save my money. I usually **spend / buy / borrow** it all at once.
3. I'm **earning / spending / saving** for a new mobile phone.
4. I want to **buy / sell / borrow** my old bike. I've got a new one now.
5. I sometimes **save / earn / spend** money by cleaning my dad's car. He gives me £2.
6. I often **borrow / save / sell** money from my sister when I want to buy something.

Your turn

6 Rewrite the sentences in Exercise 5 so they are true for you.

> 1 *I often buy clothes online but I sometimes try them on first.*

7 Ask and answer questions with the verbs in Exercise 4. Use these question beginnings.
- How often do you …?
- Are you …ing at the moment?
- Do you ever …?
- Do you usually …?

> How often do you buy clothes online?

➡ **Vocabulary bank • page 108**

Language focus 2 *(don't) want to, would(n't) like to, would prefer to*

1 Complete the examples from the listening on page 12.

Question	Answer
What do you ¹.... **to** buy?	I **want to / don't want to** buy some new shoes.
What **would** you **like to** buy?	I'd ³.... **to / wouldn't like to** buy a new games console.
².... you **prefer to** get a present?	I'**d prefer to** get some money.

➡ Grammar reference • page 100

2 🔊 **1.10** Complete the conversations with *do(n't)* or *would(n't)*. Then listen and check.

1 A: ¹.... you like to go shopping?
   B: No, I ².... prefer to stay at home.
2 A: What ³.... you want to do this afternoon?
   B: I ⁴.... like to go to the new shopping mall.
3 A: I'm saving my money at the moment. I ⁵.... like to buy a new skateboard.
   B: ⁶.... you prefer to buy it in a shop or online?
4 A: When you're older, ⁷.... you like to work in a shopping centre?
   B: No, I ⁸.... .

👁 Get it right!

Remember we use the infinitive after *would like*, NOT *-ing*.
I would like **to go** to the cinema. ✓
~~I would like going ...~~ ✗

(not) enough + noun

3 Look at these examples from the listening on page 12. Write *enough* in the correct place.

1 I'd like to buy a new games console but I haven't got money.
2 I've nearly got money.

➡ Grammar reference • page 100

➡ Say it right! • page 96

4 Rewrite the sentences with *enough*.

1 My cousin wants to buy some new sunglasses but she hasn't got money.
   My cousin wants to buy some new sunglasses but she hasn't got enough money.
2 I'd like to watch a film but I haven't got time.
3 We'd like to make hot chocolate but there isn't milk.
4 My dad thinks I don't do homework.
5 My brother is unhealthy because he doesn't do sport.
6 We want to start a football team but we haven't got players.

5 🔊 **1.11** Complete the conversations with the words in the box. Then listen and check.

enough   like   prefer   want

1 A: Would you ¹.... to go to the new shopping centre?
   B: I'm sorry I can't. I haven't got ².... money.
2 A: Do you ³.... to play football after school?
   B: I'd ⁴.... to ride my bike. I don't like ball sports.

Your turn

6 Work with a partner. Rewrite the conversations in Exercise 5 by changing the words in **bold**. Use these words or your own ideas.

go to my house   the cinema   the ice rink
a restaurant   the underwater zoo   watch a film
play tennis   have a pizza   play computer games

> Would you like to go to my house after school?

> I'm sorry I can't. I haven't got enough time.

Discover Culture

1 You are going to watch a video about a tiger charity. How do you think it helps tigers? Why is it important to help them?

Find out about a tiger sanctuary in Thailand.

1.2 Tiger sanctuary

2 ▶ 1.2 Watch the video and answer the questions.
1 What is special about the people who work at the sanctuary?
2 How do they get money to buy food for the tigers?
3 How many tigers do they have at the moment?

3 Test your memory. Which animals do you see in the video?

> monkey   bear   elephant   owl   dog   duck
> snake   bat   horse   deer   buffalo

4 ▶ 1.2 Watch the video again. Check your answers to Exercise 3 and choose the correct words.
1 Tigers go to the sanctuary when they are **ill / old** or in danger.
2 Unfortunately, some people like **hunting / hurting** tigers.
3 These tigers **can / can't** live in the wild.
4 The tigers **are / are not** like pets.
5 Everyday they **run / eat** a lot!

Your turn

5 Write answers to the questions.
1 Are there any animal sanctuaries in your country?
2 What animals do they help?
3 Do people give money to help animals?
4 What wild animals have you got in your country?

6 Work in small groups. Ask and answer the questions in Exercise 5.

> What wild animals have you got in your country?

Reading An article

1. Look at the title of the article and the photos. What happens on *Red Nose Day*?

2. 🔊 1.12 Read the article and check your ideas to Exercise 1.

3. Read the article again. Mark the sentences true (*T*) or false (*F*).
   1. Red Nose Day is every year. *False.*
   2. Everybody gives the same money.
   3. Some people wear red noses on this day.
   4. Pupils sometimes wear unusual clothes to school.
   5. In the UK, Red Nose Day helps people who need somewhere to live.
   6. Red Nose Day is a very new charity day.

Explore adjective prefixes

4. Find the opposite of *usual* in the text. How do we make it?

5. Add *un-* to the adjectives in the box. Then complete the sentences.

   | ~~usual~~ friendly fair tidy helpful happy |

   1. I like your dress. It's very different and *unusual*.
   2. You look sad. Are you …?
   3. There are things on the floor. My brother's room is …
   4. Don't ask that man to show you. He's so …
   5. They never smile or say hello. They're very …
   6. My brother gets more pocket money than me. It's …

➡ **Vocabulary bank** • page 108

Your turn

6. Write your answers to the questions. Then ask and answer them with a partner.
   1. Would you like to work for a charity? Would you prefer to help animals or people?
   2. Do you do charity events in your school? What?
   3. What would you like to do on Red Nose Day?

RED NOSE DAY! Do something funny for money!

Red Nose Day is a charity day which happens every two years in the UK. On this day, lots of people in Britain wear red noses and do something funny. They ask other people to give them money which goes to a charity to help people all over the world.

Think of something unusual you would like to do. How about having red hair for the day? Before the big day, your friends and family say how much they would like to give you to do this and later you give this money to charity.

You can do all kinds of cool things at school too. Talk to your teachers and decide together! Perhaps wear something red to school instead of your school uniform. Or play 'red nose day' games instead of having normal lessons?

And where does this money go? In the UK, it can help to find homes for young people who are living on the street. In Africa, the money can buy important medicine or give fresh water to villages.

FACT! Red Nose Day is over 25 years old. In 25 years people have given more than £100,000,000!

Speaking Shopping

Real talk: How do you spend your money?

1 ▶ 1.3 Watch the teenagers in the video. How do they spend their money? Use these words.

| phone   food   music   going out with friends   clothes   comic books   concert tickets   video games |

a) Speaker 1 ..food..   c) Speaker 3 ....   e) Speaker 5 .... and ....
b) Speaker 2 ....   d) Speaker 4 ....   f) Speaker 6 .... and ....

2 💬 How do *you* spend your money? Ask and answer with your partner.

3 🔊 1.13 Listen to Matt talking to a shop assistant. What colour trainers would he like?

4 🔊 1.13 Complete the conversation with the useful language. Then listen and check your answers.

Useful language

Can I try them on?   What size are you?
How much are they?   I'd prefer …
I'd like to buy …   I'll take them!

Matt:	Excuse me, ¹.... some **trainers**.
Shop assistant:	What about these?
Matt:	².... a different colour. Have you got anything in **blue**?
Shop assistant:	Yes, do you like these?
Matt:	Yes! ³....
Shop assistant:	They're **£59.99**.
Matt:	⁴....
Shop assistant:	Of course. ⁵....
Matt:	I'm a size **40**, I think.
Shop assistant:	Here you are.
Shop assistant:	How are they?
Matt:	They're great. ⁶....

5 💬 Practise the conversation in Exercise 4 with a partner.

6 💬 Change the words in **bold** in the conversation in Exercise 4. Use the pictures below or your own ideas. Then, practise the conversation.

size 38 €20   medium €35   size 36 €45

Excuse me, I'd like to buy some jeans.

What about these?

Writing An email

1 Look at the photo and read the emails. What help does Joey give Annie?

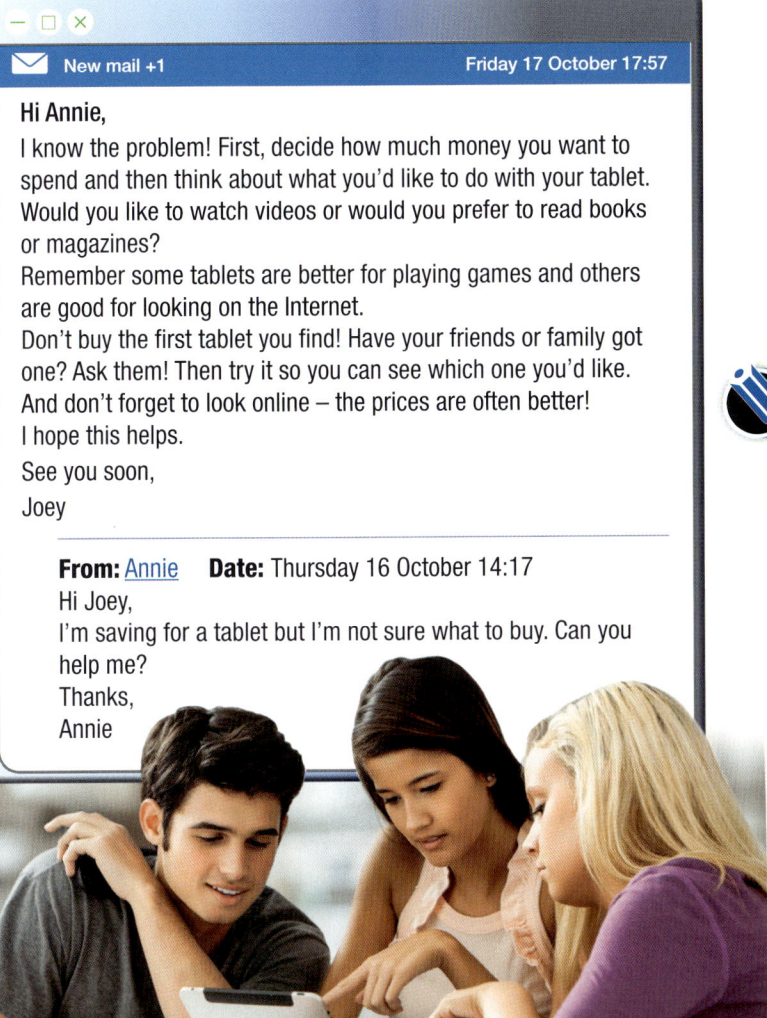

> **New mail +1** Friday 17 October 17:57
>
> Hi Annie,
> I know the problem! First, decide how much money you want to spend and then think about what you'd like to do with your tablet. Would you like to watch videos or would you prefer to read books or magazines?
> Remember some tablets are better for playing games and others are good for looking on the Internet.
> Don't buy the first tablet you find! Have your friends or family got one? Ask them! Then try it so you can see which one you'd like. And don't forget to look online – the prices are often better!
> I hope this helps.
> See you soon,
> Joey
>
> **From:** Annie   **Date:** Thursday 16 October 14:17
> Hi Joey,
> I'm saving for a tablet but I'm not sure what to buy. Can you help me?
> Thanks,
> Annie

2 Order the things Joey does in his email.
   a make a suggestion
   b begin the email *1*
   c give some information
   d end the email
   e respond to the previous email

3 Find the words Joey uses to do the things in Exercise 2.
   1 *begin the email – Hi Annie,*

Useful language

Imperatives
In an email, we often make suggestions. Use the imperative for a quick, informal way to do this:
- *Decide how much money you want to spend.*
- *Don't buy the first tablet you find.*

4 Find five more examples of imperatives in Joey's email.

5 Complete the sentences with the imperatives from the box.

> Don't buy   Go   Read   Save   Try

1 …. your friends' tablets to see which one you'd like.
2 …. to an electronics shop and ask for advice.
3 …. reviews of new tablets.
4 …. enough money to buy a good tablet.
5 …. anything online if it is really cheap – it's probably not very good.

Get Writing

PLAN

6 Read the email from Danny and make notes about what you want to say. Use the ideas in Exercise 2.

> **New mail +1**
>
> Hi,
> My parents would like to give me a laptop but we aren't sure what to buy or where to buy it. They want to go to the department store but I'd prefer to buy it online.
> What do you think?
> Danny

WRITE

7 Write your email. Use your notes and the language below.

Hi
I know the problem.
First, … and then …
Would you like to … or would you prefer to …?
I hope this helps.
See you soon,

CHECK

8 Can you say YES to these questions?
- Have you got imperatives to make suggestions?
- Have you got the information from Exercise 2?
- Have you got the language from Exercise 7?

2 Our heroes

Discovery EDUCATION

In this unit ...

Wildlife hero **p21**

The Chilean Mine Rescue **p24**

Role models **p26**

CLIL Amelia Earhart, famous flyer **p117**

Vocabulary
- Jobs
- Adjectives of character
- Expressions with *make*
- The suffix *-ness*

Language focus
- *was/were*
- past simple: affirmative and negative
- past simple time expressions
- *was/were* and past simple questions

Unit aims
I can ...
- talk about different jobs.
- describe events in the past.
- understand information about present and past heroes.
- ask and answer questions about things in the past.
- give an opinion about something I'm not sure about.
- write a description of a person.

BE CURIOUS

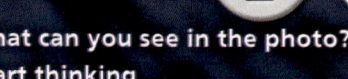

What can you see in the photo?
Start thinking
- What do you think happened before this photo?
- Who is the hero in the photo and why?
- Who are your heroes?

Vocabulary Jobs

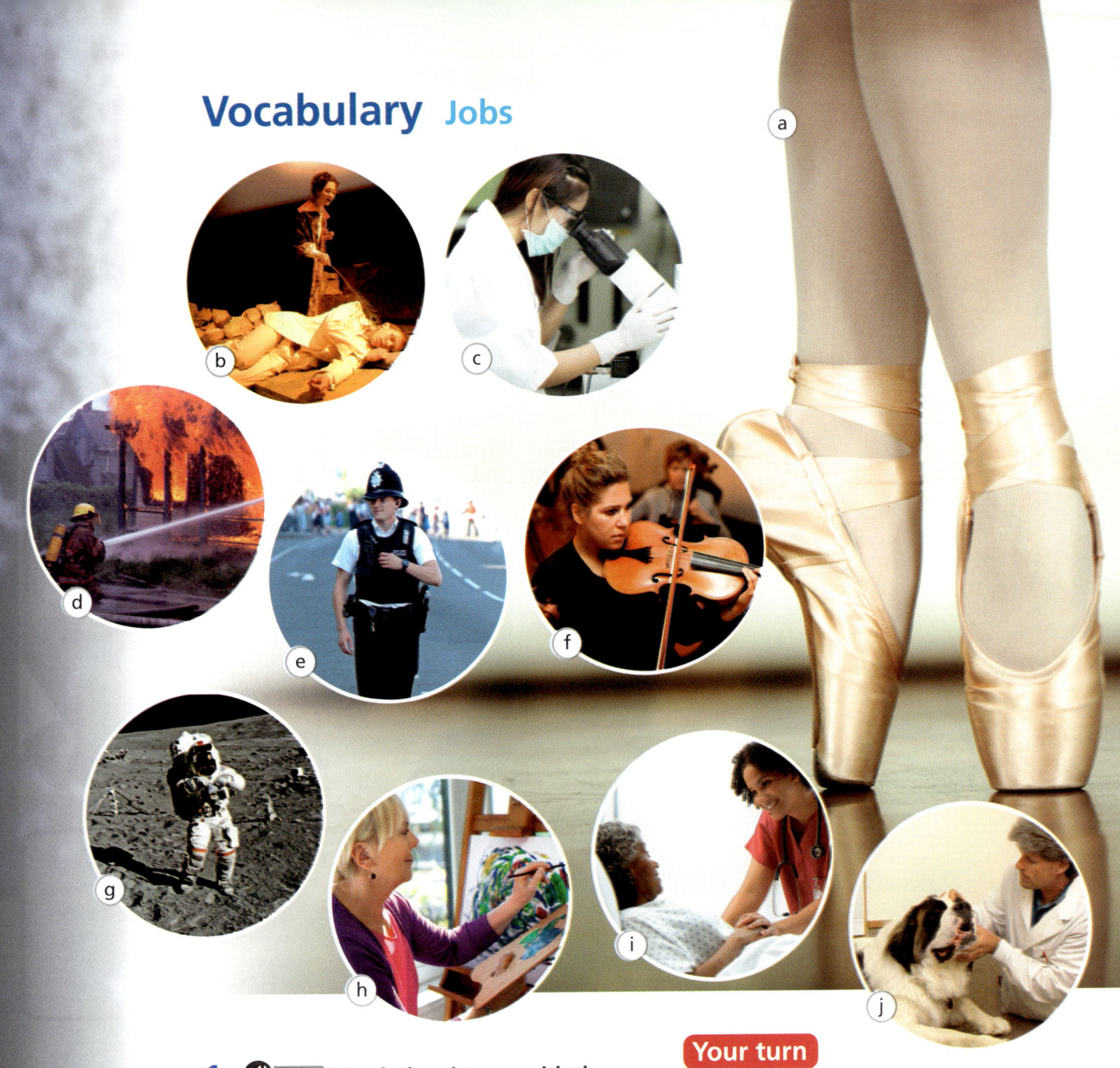

1 🔊 1.14 Match the pictures with the words in the box. Then listen, check and repeat.

> dancer   police officer   musician   actor
> nurse   artist   vet   astronaut   scientist
> firefighter

2 Complete the table with the words in Exercise 1.

Science	Artistic / Creative	Life savers
scientist		

Your turn

3 Look at the jobs in Exercise 1 and write answers to the questions.
1 Which two jobs would you like to do? Why?
2 Which two jobs would you not like to do? Why?

I'd like to be an artist because I love drawing and painting.

4 Work with a partner. Ask and answer the questions in Exercise 3.

> Which job would you like to do?

> I'd like to be an artist because I love drawing and painting. What about you?

➡ Vocabulary bank • page 109

QUIZ OF THE MONTH

PEOPLE WHO MADE A DIFFERENCE

1 Christopher Columbus was born in Genoa over 500 years ago. He wanted to sail to Asia from Europe. He started his journey in 1492, but he didn't arrive in Asia because he made a mistake. Two months later he arrived in …..

- **A** The Caribbean Islands
- **B** Brazil
- **C** Canada

2 Anne Frank was a young Jewish girl living in Amsterdam over 80 years ago. During the Second World War, her family hid in a few small rooms in a house because the German army wanted to put Jewish people in prison. They were there for two years. Every day, Anne wrote about her life. In 1944, the Germans found Anne and her family and took them to Germany where she died in March 1945. What is the name of the book that she wrote?

- **A** My Life at War
- **B** A Girl's Life
- **C** The Diary of a Young Girl

3 Tim Berners-Lee was an engineer but became interested in computers in the 1970s. He wrote a program that could connect computers across the world. He called it the World Wide Web and made history when he gave it to the world for free. He said, 'This is for everyone.' But when did the web go worldwide?

- **A** in 1980
- **B** in 1991
- **C** in 2002

> **FACT!** Teachers can be heroes too. In 2012, Elaine Johnson, a primary school teacher from California, USA saved the lives of two students when she pulled them from a car that was on fire. Amazingly, the students weren't hurt.

Reading A magazine quiz

1 Look at the people in the pictures. Who are they? Why are they famous?

2 🔊 1.15 Read the quiz and check your answers to Exercise 1.

3 Read the quiz again and answer the questions.

Explore expressions with *make*

4 Find three expressions with *make* in the text.

5 Complete the sentences with *make* and one of the words in the box.

> a cake   ~~mistakes~~   friends   a suggestion   history   sure

1. Do the exam carefully. Try not to _make mistakes_.
2. When I go on holiday, I often …. with the new people I meet.
3. People who change something in our world …. .
4. It's John's birthday tomorrow. Let's …. .
5. Before you close the door, …. you've got your keys.
6. Can I …. ? Let's go to the cinema on Saturday afternoon.

➡ **Vocabulary bank** • page 109

Your turn

6 Think of a famous hero. Write your answers to the questions.
1. What's his/her name?
2. Where is he/she from?
3. Where does he/she live?
4. What does he/she do?
5. Why is he/she a hero?

7 Work with a partner. Ask and answer the questions about your hero in Exercise 6.

> What's your hero's name?

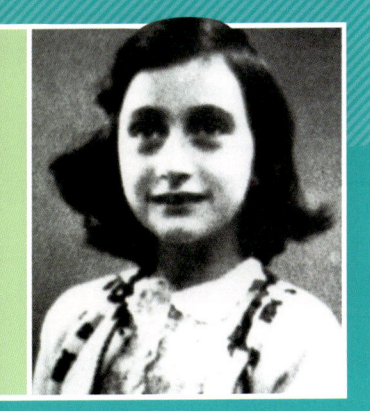

Language focus 1 *was/were*

1 Complete the examples from the text on page 20.

	I / he / she / it	you / we / they
+	Anne Frank ¹.... a young Jewish girl.	They ².... there for two years.
–	America **wasn't** on Columbus' map.	Amazingly, the students ³.... hurt.

➡ Grammar reference • page 101

2 Choose the correct answer.
1 He **was / were / weren't** a famous tennis player 10 years ago.
2 You **were / wasn't / was** very good at sport at primary school.
3 I **were / weren't / was** at home at 8 o'clock last night.
4 My friends **were / was / wasn't** at football practice yesterday.
5 I **were / weren't / wasn't** at school last week. I **was / were / weren't** ill.
6 She **was / were / weren't** born in Ireland in 1991.

Past simple and time expressions

3 Complete the examples from the text on page 20.

+	He ¹.... his journey in 1492.
–	He ².... arrive in Asia.

➡ Grammar reference • page 101

➡ Say it right! • page 96

4 Complete the sentences in the past simple with the words in brackets.
1 I usually do my homework before dinner but yesterday, *I did my homework* (after dinner).
2 We normally have our lunch at school but on Monday .... (at home).
3 I often swim in the swimming pool but last summer, ... (in the lake).
4 I visit my grandparents on Sundays but last weekend .... (on Saturday).
5 My mum teaches at my brother's school but when I was little .... (at my school).
6 I study in the library every day now but three years ago I .... (once a week).

5 Complete the text with the verbs in brackets.

Marie Curie ¹.... (be) a scientist. She ².... (live) in Paris, France but she ³.... (not be) French, she ⁴.... (be) from Poland. She ⁵.... (meet) her husband, Pierre, at university in Paris, and together they ⁶.... (discover) radium. Many of the teachers at the university ⁷.... (not want) Marie to teach there because she was a woman, but in 1906 she ⁸.... (make) history and ⁹.... (become) the first woman to teach at the university, three years after becoming the first woman to win a Nobel prize.

6 Order the time expressions in the box. Start with the most recent.

> yesterday   this morning   when I was little
> four days ago   last weekend

Your turn

7 Think of some people you know. Write sentences about what they did and when. Use the events below and the time expressions in Exercise 6. Then compare your sentences with your partner.

> went to school   gave me a present
> played a sport   helped me   went to a party
> read a book   went to a foreign country   was ill

My best friend went to school this morning.

Learn about Yanna, a vet in South Africa.
• Why is Yanna's job special?
• Why did she become a vet?
• Why did she shoot the rhino in the video?

2.1 Wildlife hero

Listening A conversation

1 Look at the advertisement. What is Young Heroes?

2 🔊 1.18 Listen to Laura talking to Harry and check your answer to Exercise 1.

3 🔊 1.18 Listen again and answer the questions.
   1 Who do they give prizes to?
   2 How did the programme choose the winners?
   3 What did Mike do last year?
   4 What does Lisa do for other young people?
   5 Is Alan still ill?
   6 What does Alan do when he isn't studying?

Young Heroes

CHANNEL 5   7 PM – 9 PM

Tonight we give a special prize to three young heroes. Live music from One Direction and Beyoncé.

Vocabulary Adjectives of character

4 🔊 1.19 Look at the pictures and complete the sentences with the words in the box. Then listen and check.

brave   calm   cheerful   friendly   funny   kind   quiet   serious

1 Steven is very ..... . He didn't say anything in class today.

5 Alice is so ..... . When we went on holiday together, she was happy every day and smiled at everyone.

2 Becky's really ..... . She made us laugh a lot at the party.

6 Jack was ..... when the accident happened. He wasn't afraid and he called the police.

3 Ben's very ..... . We went to see a funny film and he didn't laugh at all.

7 Andy is really ..... . He made lots of new friends at summer camp.

4 Anna's really ..... . She went on everything at the theme park!

8 Tania is very ..... to animals. She gave a cat some food last week, and then she found it a home.

Your turn

5 Use the adjectives in Exercise 4 to write sentences about five people you know.
   My little sister is brave. Last week, she caught three mice and six spiders.

6 Work with a partner. Read your sentences from Exercise 5 but don't say the adjective. Can your partner guess the adjective?
   A: *Last week, my sister caught three mice and six spiders.*
   B: *She's brave!*

➡ Vocabulary bank • page 109

Language focus 2 was/were: questions

1 Complete the examples from the listening on page 22.

	I / he / she / it	you / we / they
Wh-	Who ¹.... the third hero?	Who ².... the winners?
Y/N ?	**Was** the show good?	**Were** you at school?
Short answers	Yes, it **was**. No, it **wasn't**.	Yes, we **were**. No, we **weren't**.

➡ Grammar reference • page 101

2 Order the words to make questions with *was* and *were*.
1 at this time yesterday / Where / you / were?
2 time / you / at / were / this / school / What / morning?
3 were / at / Who / friends / primary / your / school?
4 born / you / When / were?
5 teacher / was / first / Who / your / English?
6 your / was / five / ago / favourite / What / TV programme / years?

3 Work with a partner. Ask and answer the questions in Exercise 2.

Past simple: questions

4 Complete the examples from the listening on page 22.

	I / he / she / it	you / we / they
Wh- ?	What **did** she ¹....?	How **did** they ².... them?
Y/N ?	**Did** he **win**?	³.... you **watch** TV last night?
Short answers	Yes, he **did**. No, he **didn't**.	Yes, you **did**. No, you **didn't**.

➡ Grammar reference • page 101

> 👁 **Get it right!**
> Use the infinitive without *to* with *did* in past simple questions and negatives:
> What **did** you **eat** yesterday? ✓
> ~~What **did** you **ate** yesterday?~~ ✗
> I **didn't see** my cousin at the party. ✓
> ~~I **didn't saw** my cousin at the party.~~ ✗

5 Read the answers. Then complete the questions.
1 What ..*did*.. you ..*have*.. for breakfast?
   I had toast and hot chocolate.
2 Where .... you .... your shoes?
   I bought them in the department store.
3 What time .... your mother .... home?
   She came home at 8 o'clock.
4 Who .... you .... to school with?
   I walked with my friends.
5 Where .... your parents .... before?
   They lived in Paris.
6 What .... your teacher .... at university?
   She studied Maths.

6 Write questions in the past simple.
1 When / you / start secondary school?
   When did you start secondary school?
2 Who / you / meet at the weekend?
3 Where / you / go on holiday last summer?
4 What / your family / watch on TV last night?
5 How / you / get to school this morning?
6 What sports / you / play yesterday?

Your turn

7 Write your answers to the questions in Exercise 6.
1 *I started it three years ago.*

8 Work with a partner. Ask and answer the questions in Exercise 6. Remember to ask for more information.

> When did you start secondary school?

> I started three years ago.

> Did you enjoy the first day?

> Yes, I did because I made some new friends.

Discover Culture

1 Look at the picture. What job do you think the men do? Can you guess why they are heroes?

Find out about a mine rescue in Chile.

2.2 The Chilean Mine Rescue

2 ▶ 2.2 Watch the video and check your answers to Exercise 1. Then choose the correct options in the text below.

In ¹2010 / 2012, there was a terrible accident. A giant rock fell and closed the San José mine with ²33 / 43 miners inside. Luckily, the miners found a safe place ³70 / 700 metres underground. The rescue workers made lots of holes to try to find the miners. Finally, ⁴69 / 79 days after the accident, the first man came out alive. The rescue worked. These brave men were suddenly ⁵national / international heroes.

3 Test your memory. Complete the sentences.
1 The San José Mine is in the Atacama …
2 The rock fell in front of the mine's …
3 The camp was called *Esperanza* which means …
4 The families knew the miners were OK because they wrote a …
5 Families could see the miners because they had a …
6 A million people all over the world watched the final …

4 ▶ 2.2 Test your memory. Put the images in the order you see them in the video. Then watch again and check your answers.
1 Rescue workers talk to the miners on the phone
2 The desert from the sky
3 A miner in hospital
4 The families' camp with posters and flags
5 The families hold flags and celebrate
6 A message on the drill

Your turn

5 Work with a partner. Imagine you are journalists and you are going to interview the Chilean miners. Write questions in the past with the question words and verbs below or your own ideas.

> What   Who   When   How   Where

> eat   drink   play   sleep   read
> talk   write   walk   feel

What did you eat? Did you play games?

6 Work in small groups. Journalists ask your questions from Exercise 5 and miners answer. Then swap.

> What did you eat?

> We had a little cold food with us. Then the rescue workers gave us some more food.

Reading A blog

1 Look at the map and the photos. Where is Jamaica? Who are the people in the photos?

2 🔊 1.20 Read Danielle's blog and check your answers to Exercise 1.

3 Read the article again and answer the questions.
1. How many people live in Jamaica?
2. What sorts of heroes does Danielle write about?
3. When do Jamaican children start doing sport at school?
4. What or who is *Champs*?
5. What type of music started in Jamaica?
6. What do Jamaican musicians often sing about?

Explore the suffix *-ness*

4 Look at the article again. Find the noun from the adjectives *happy* and *sad*. Then answer the questions.
1. What do we add to the adjective to make the noun?
2. What happens to the 'y' in *happy* when we make the noun?

5 Complete the sentences with the noun of the adjective in brackets.
1. Many musicians write songs about love and ...*sadness*... . (sad)
2. Please put your books on the shelf. .... is very important. (tidy)
3. I think .... is more important than money. (happy)
4. Singing is my .... . I'm not very good at it. (weak)
5. The band didn't play because of .... . (ill)
6. I'll never forget my grandma's .... when she listened to my problems. (kind)

➡ **Vocabulary bank • page 109**

Your turn

6 Write your answers to the questions. Then ask and answer them with a partner.
1. Who's your favourite sportsperson? Where's he/she from? What sports does he/she do?
2. Who's your favourite musician? Where's he/she from? What kind of music does he/she play?

DANIELLE SMITH'S BLOG OF ALL THINGS JAMAICAN

A SMALL ISLAND FULL OF BIG HEROES

14 OCTOBER

I live on the small Caribbean island of Jamaica. Like many of the 3 million people here, sport and music are very important to me. Perhaps that's why so many sports and music heroes come from our island.

We start playing sports seriously at a very young age. Even at primary school we follow an athletics programme. At secondary school, there's the school athletics championship, or 'Champs'. Every year, about 25,000 people watch some of the heroes of tomorrow. Usain Bolt, the Olympic Gold Medallist, is from Jamaica and he once entered this championship.

As for music, in the 1960s, my own hero Bob Marley introduced reggae to the world. He didn't only sing about happiness, love and sadness. He also sang about how people live and their problems. Today, even our youngest musicians write about our life here on the island. When you next listen to a song from Jamaica, don't forget it's probably about us, our life and our culture!

FACT! The Jamaican bobsleigh team became heroes when they entered the Winter Olympics in 1988. Strange! Jamaica is famous for its sun but not for its snow!

Speaking Speculating

Real talk: Who's your role model and why?

1 ▶ 2.3 Watch the teenagers in the video and match them with their role models.

a) Speaker 1   1 a friend because he saved his sister from a fire.
b) Speaker 2   2 a famous actor because she's good at her job and helps children.
c) Speaker 3   3 a teacher because her lessons are really interesting.
d) Speaker 4   4 an athlete because he can run fast.
e) Speaker 5   5 someone in his family because he's kind and hardworking.
f) Speaker 6   6 someone in her family because she dances well.

2 Who's *your* role model and why? Ask and answer with your partner.

3 🔊 1.21 Listen to Darren and Louise talking about the woman in the photo above. What job do they think she does?

4 🔊 1.21 Complete the conversation with the useful language. Then listen again and check your answers.

Useful language

She looks (very kind).   She definitely (works with
… that's possible.   animals).
She may be (a vet).   I reckon she's (a vet).

5 Work with a partner. Practise the conversation in Exercise 4.

6 Work with a partner. Prepare a conversation like the one in Exercise 4. Use the photos below and the useful language. Practise the conversation with your partner.

Darren:	What do you think she does?
Louise:	I'm not sure.
Darren:	¹… very kind.
Louise:	Yes, and friendly.
Darren:	²… an artist.
Louise:	Yes, ³… . Or she may be a vet because there's a gorilla in the photo.
Darren:	Yes, that's true. ⁴… works with animals.
Louise:	Yes, ⁵… a vet or a scientist.
Darren:	Me too.
Louise:	Let's ask the teacher.

Writing A description of a person you admire

1 Look at the photo and read Jennifer's description. Is Jennifer's hero famous?

Although most people have got heroes like Nelson Mandela or Usain Bolt, my hero is my granddad. He was born 80 years ago so he's very old. When he was a young boy, his parents died so he lived with his aunt, uncle and cousins in Manchester. Life wasn't easy for them because they never had enough money.

When he was 13, my granddad left school and started working. He wanted to be a vet so he studied at night after work as well. He worked really hard and he became a vet when he was 25. It was his dream job.

I like him because he's funny, friendly and kind to everyone, and I admire him because he worked hard to achieve his dream.

I would like to be like him when I'm older.

By Jennifer Thompson

2 Read Jennifer's description and answer the questions.
1 Who is Jennifer's hero?
2 Where did he live?
3 What was his job?
4 Why is he a hero?
5 What's her hero like?

Useful language

Connectors
We often use connectors when we write descriptions:
- *Although* most people have got heroes like Nelson Mandela or Usain Bolt, my hero is my granddad.
- *I like him because he's funny, friendly and kind to everyone.*
- *He was born 80 years ago so he's very old.*
- *He wanted to be a vet so he studied at night after work as well.*

3 Complete the sentences with *as well, although, because* or *so*.
1 My hero is my teacher .... I learn a lot in her class.
2 They help with the local football team and organise the youth club .... .
3 My best friend helped me when I was having problems .... I'm going to buy her a present.
4 My aunt gives a lot of money to charities .... she never talks about it.
5 I would like to be a vet .... I like helping animals.
6 David wants to go to university .... he doesn't know which one to go to.

Get Writing

PLAN

4 Make notes about a person you admire. Use the questions in Exercise 2.

WRITE

5 Write your description. Use your notes from Exercise 4, and the language below.

My hero is …
He/She was born …
When he/she was …
I like him/her because …
I admire him/her because …
I would like to be like him/her when I'm older.

CHECK

6 Can you say YES to these questions?
- Have you got connectors to add more information?
- Have you got the information from Exercise 4?
- Have you got the language from Exercise 5?

1–2 Review

Vocabulary

1 Match the pictures with the shops in the box.

> sports shop   chemist   electronics shop
> clothes shop   newsagent   music shop

2 Complete the sentences with the words in the box.

> borrow   buy   earn   save   sell   spend

1 I'm going to the bookshop to …. a book.
2 My brother wants to …. his old laptop for €50.
3 Can I …. some money? I can give it back to you tomorrow!
4 How much money do you …. on sweets every week?
5 I sometimes help my dad in the garden to …. extra pocket money.
6 I'm not eating sweets because I'm trying to …. money for a new bike.

3 Look at the pictures and write the jobs.

4 Match the sentences with the adjectives.

> calm   cheerful   funny   brave   quiet   serious

1 I'm not scared of spiders, big dogs or dentists. I'm …. .
2 My classmate Max never laughs. He's very …. .
3 I'm a nervous person and I worry about things. I'm not very …. .
4 My uncle is really good at telling jokes. He's very …. .
5 My sister talks a lot. It's difficult for her to be …. .
6 My little sister always smiles and laughs. She's very …. .

Explore vocabulary

5 Choose the correct answers.

1 I'm wearing two sweaters, a coat and gloves because it's **freezing / awful**.
2 That new shopping centre has got more than 1,000 shops. It's **huge / boiling**.
3 I didn't like that new restaurant. The food was **brilliant / awful**.
4 We can't play football because it's 36°C outside. It's **brilliant / boiling**.
5 I loved the concert. I thought the singer was **brilliant / freezing**.

6 Complete the sentences. Add the prefix *un-* or the suffix *-ness* to the words in brackets.

1 I never go to that shop because the shop assistants are very …. . (helpful)
2 Why has Jack got a bigger piece of cake? That's …. . (fair)
3 I think …. is very important in a friend. (kind)
4 I would like to earn a lot of money but …. is more important. (happy)
5 It's May and it's snowing! That's …. . (usual)
6 My teacher says that …. is very important. I don't agree. (tidy)

7 Complete the sentences with the correct form of *make* and one of these words.

> sure   a cake   friends   history
> a suggestion   mistakes

1 When you leave the house, …. you've got your keys.
2 I'd like to …. . Why don't you try on those shoes before you buy them?
3 My friends always do their homework quickly so they …. .
4 We haven't got enough eggs. We can't …. .
5 I'm a friendly person so I …. very easily.
6 I'd love to do something important for the world and …. .

28

UNIT 1–2

Language focus

1 Complete the text with the present continuous form of the verbs in brackets.

Lisa and Clare ¹.... (not study) today. They ².... (shop). They ³.... (look) for new dresses for a party on Saturday. Lisa ⁴.... (try) on a red dress. Clare ⁵.... (not try) on dresses at the moment. She ⁶.... (take) a photo of a dress to send to her mum.

2 Complete the sentences with the present simple or present continuous form of the verbs in brackets.

1. We .... History at the moment. (study)
2. What time .... he usually .... to school? (go)
3. My parents often .... TV in the evening. (watch)
4. Peter and Susana .... for clothes right now. (shop)
5. .... you .... dinner now? (eat)
6. They .... to the cinema every weekend. (not go)

3 Choose the correct answers.

1. A: Would you ¹**want / like** to have a pizza before we go home?
   B: I'm sorry I can't. I haven't got ²**enough time / time enough**.
2. A: I ³**wouldn't / don't** want to go to the ice rink.
   B: I agree. I'd ⁴**prefer / want** to go to the cinema.
3. A: I haven't got ⁵**enough money / money enough** to go to the underwater zoo.
   B: Don't worry. I don't ⁶**like / want** to go there today.

4 Complete the text with the correct past simple form of the verbs in the box.

> buy   go   move   leave   be (x4)   want
> not be   not live   study

Joanna ¹.... born in Canada, but she ².... there for very long. When she ³.... three, her parents ⁴.... to England. They ⁵.... a house in South London. Joanna ⁶.... to school in Chelsea. Unfortunately, she ⁷.... very good at subjects like Science and Maths, but she ⁸.... good at Art. When she ⁹.... school, she ¹⁰.... Art and Design at university. Her parents ¹¹.... a little sad at first – they ¹².... her to be a doctor. But now they're happy because she's happy!

5 Complete the questions with *was*, *were* or *did*.

1. Where .... you born?
2. What languages .... Lisa study?
3. When .... you go to France?
4. .... you study Biology at school?
5. .... Mike good at Maths?
6. .... your parents at home last night?

6 Complete the sentences with the time expressions in the box.

> last night   an hour ago   when I was little
> at the weekend   yesterday

1. I had lunch at 1 pm, now it's 2 pm. I had lunch ..... .
2. Jack started school on Monday. Today is Tuesday. He started school ..... .
3. Helen was at home on Saturday and Sunday. She was at home ..... .
4. I watched the film yesterday at 8 pm. I watched the film ..... .
5. We moved here in 2006. I was 4 years old. We moved here ..... .

Language builder

7 Choose the correct answers.

Nina: Hi, Debbie. ¹ _b_ anything at the moment?
Debbie: No, not really. Why?
Nina: They ².... a market at the sports centre today. ³.... you like to come with me?
Debbie: Yes, please! I ⁴.... markets. I ⁵.... interesting things.
Nina: Me too! I went to a market two weeks ⁶.... and I ⁷.... a baseball cap and some sunglasses.
Debbie: ⁸.... they expensive?
Nina: No, not at all. I ⁹.... spend more than £10. I wanted to buy some trainers but I didn't have ¹⁰..... .

1	a Do you do	b Are you doing
2	a 're having	b have
3	a Would	b Do
4	a love	b loves
5	a often find	b 'm often finding
6	a past	b ago
7	a am buying	b bought
8	a Were	b Did
9	a didn't	b wasn't
10	a money enough	b enough money

Speaking

8 Complete the phrases with the words in the box.

> looks   possible   think   may   reckon   sure

1. What do you .... she does?
2. I'm not ..... .
3. She .... be a nurse.
4. She .... very kind.
5. I .... she's a teacher.
6. That's ..... .

3 Strange stories

In this unit ...

Mystery in the mountains **p33**

A story from under the sea **p36**

Strange events **p38**

CLIL Behind the scenes **p118**

Vocabulary
- Action verbs
- Adverbs of manner
- Expressions with *look*
- Nouns with *-er*

Language focus
- Past continuous
- Past continuous vs. past simple
- could(n't)

Unit aims
I can ...
- tell a story using action verbs.
- understand strange stories.
- talk about my activities in the past.
- describe how I do things.
- talk about the things I could and couldn't do when I was younger.
- tell someone my news.
- write a story.

BE CURIOUS

What can you see in the photo?
Start thinking
- Do you think this is a real photo? Why/Why not?
- What other strange things do you know about?
- Can you think of an explanation for these mysteries?

Vocabulary Action verbs

1 Look at the story about a thief. What did the thief steal?

2 🔊 1.22 Match the pictures with the words in the box. Then listen, check and repeat.

> catch   chase   climb   hide   fall over
> jump   run away   throw

3 Complete the sentences with the past simple form of the verbs in Exercise 2.
1. The thief ..*ran*.. away from our car.
2. I .... the thief.
3. The thief .... into a garden.
4. The thief .... his bag over a wall.
5. The thief .... over a wall.
6. The thief .... the bag.
7. The thief .... .
8. I .... the thief.

Your turn

4 Work with a partner. Cover the sentences in Exercise 3. Then ask and answer questions about the story.

> What happened in picture 1?

> The thief ran away from the car.

5 Cover the pictures and write down the 8 sentences about the story.

➤ **Vocabulary bank** • page 110

Reading A newspaper article

1 Work with a partner. Look at the pictures. What do you think happened in the story?

2 🔊 1.23 Read the newspaper article and check your ideas to Exercise 1.

HOME   WORLD   UK   BUSINESS   EDUCATION

TREASURE IN THE PARK

Pupils from Parkland School in Leeds were surprised last week when they were cleaning the park. They were looking for rubbish when they found something that looked like treasure!

'I was looking after their bags when I heard someone shout by the lake. I ran over and one of the children was jumping and pointing at a large bag. They weren't laughing but they were really excited,' said their teacher, Mrs Gibson. 'I phoned the police immediately.'

The police looked in the bag. It was full of expensive objects like watches and clocks, and even some gold. There were also some old photos, a Hungarian passport, two train tickets to Berlin and an old newspaper from 1956.

But where did these things come from? Who did they belong to? What were they doing there?

Police detective Stuart Bolan said, 'This morning I spoke to police in Hungary and they are trying to find the owner of the passport. The bag was in the park for a very long time so it really is a mystery.'

Were the children still talking about it a week later? 'They are very excited and are going to do a project on what they found,' said Mrs Gibson.

3 Read the text again and answer the questions.
1 What school did the children go to?
2 Where did they find the treasure?
3 What did the teacher do when she saw the bag?
4 Who opened the bag?
5 What was inside the bag?
6 Who did the police speak to about the objects?

Explore expressions with *look*

4 Find four examples of *look* + preposition in the newspaper article. Then complete the sentences with the correct preposition.
1 I was looking ...*for*... my keys, when I found my mobile phone.
2 Can you look .... the kitchen for my bag?
3 My aunt is working so I'm looking .... my little cousin.
4 I'm not sure what it is but it looks .... an old boot.

➡ **Vocabulary bank • page 110**

Your turn

5 Look at the text. Write your own answers to the three questions in bold in the fourth paragraph.

6 Work in small groups. Compare your answers to the questions in Exercise 5 and decide which is your favourite.

> I think thieves stole these objects.

> I agree. But where did they come from?

FACT! *Four months before the 1966 World Cup in England, a thief stole the World Cup trophy and hid it inside some newspaper at the bottom of a garden. A dog called Pickles found it seven days later while he was walking with his owner. Both Pickles and his owner received a reward!*

Language focus 1 Past continuous: affirmative and negative

1 Complete the examples from the text on page 32.

	I / he / she / it	you / we / they
+	I ¹.... **looking** after their bags.	They **were** ².... for rubbish.
–	I **wasn't watching** the children.	They ³.... **laughing**.

➜ Grammar reference • page 102

2 Complete the police report with the past continuous form of the verbs in brackets.

```
POLICE REPORT

Case No: 76543
Date and Time: 21 May 11 am

Police officer: Alfred Baker
Name of witness: Jim Hanson

Information:
What were you doing at the time?
When my friends found the bag, I
¹was climbing (climb) a tree and Danny
².... (hide) behind that wall because
Max ³.... (chase) us. Our teacher ⁴....
(stand) over there. She wasn't happy
with us because we ⁵.... (not help)
the others. Our classmates ⁶.... (not
play), they ⁷.... (look) for rubbish
and they ⁸.... (throw) empty cans and
bottles into a bag.
```

Past continuous: questions

3 Complete the examples from the text on page 32.

	I / he / she / it	you / we / they
Wh- ?	What **was** Danny **doing**?	What **were** they ¹.... there?
Y/N ?	**Was** she **looking** after the bag?	².... the children still **talking** about it?
Short answers	Yes, she **was**. No, she **wasn't**.	Yes, they **were**. No, they **weren't**.

➜ Grammar reference • page 102

4 🔊 **1.24** Complete the conversation with the past continuous form of the verbs in brackets. Then listen and check your answers.

Detective:	What ¹ _were_ you _doing_ (do) between 8 and 8.30 last night?
Schoolboy:	I ².... (look) at my Maths book.
Detective:	Why ³.... you .... (study) Maths?
Schoolboy:	Because I've got an exam tomorrow.
Detective:	Where ⁴.... you .... (sit)?
Schoolboy:	In my bedroom.
Detective:	⁵.... you .... (talk) to anyone at the same time?
Schoolboy:	No, I ⁶.... (do) it alone.

➜ Say it right! • page 96

Your turn

5 Write questions for your partner with the past continuous. Use these times or your own ideas.

> 5 pm   last Wednesday   2 pm on Saturday
> yesterday   11 am   last night   7 pm
> 8 am this morning

What were you doing at 2 pm on Saturday?
Were you having lunch?

6 Work with a partner. Ask and answer your questions from Exercise 5.

> What were you doing at 2 pm on Saturday?

> I was finishing my homework.

Learn about an archaeologist's discovery.
• What did the archaeologist and his team find?
• What did he discover about the woman?
• Why do you think she travelled so far?

3.1 Mystery in the mountains

Listening A strange story

1 Look at Liz's status update and the pictures. Why did Liz say "Goodbye Granny" in the shop?

Liz Matthews posted 45 minutes ago
Don't say "Goodbye Granny" to the old lady in the cake shop!!

2 🔊 1.25 Listen to Liz telling her friend Mel what happened to her. Check your ideas to Exercise 1.

3 🔊 1.25 Listen again. Mark the sentences true (*T*) or false (*F*).
1 Liz's brother's birthday is today.
2 When Liz got to the shop, it was empty.
3 An old lady started talking to Liz outside the cake shop.
4 Liz paid £17 for the cake.
5 Liz bought her cake and the cakes for the old lady too.

Vocabulary Adverbs of manner

4 Look at the examples from the listening and answer the questions.
- An old lady was standing **quietly** next to me …
- The others were talking **loudly**.
1 Are the words in bold adjectives or adverbs?
2 What do we usually add to adjectives to make adverbs?

Get it right!
Remember these adverbs are irregular:
good → well, fast → fast, hard → hard

Your turn

6 Write your answers to the questions.
1 Do you always do your homework carefully?
2 Can you speak English well?
3 Do you get dressed for school quickly?
4 Is there anything you do badly?
5 Do you always speak in class quietly?
6 What can you do easily?

7 Work with a partner. Ask and answer the questions from Exercise 6.

➡ Vocabulary bank • page 110

5 🔊 1.26 Complete the sentences with the correct form of the adjectives in brackets. Then listen, check and repeat.

a. He cooks very *badly* (bad).

b. The insect moved …. (slow) across the leaf.

c. I carried the expensive glasses very …. (careful).

d. The children were playing very …. (happy).

e. I got dressed …. (quick) and went out.

f. She answered all of the questions …. (easy).

g. He paints very …. (good).

h. She opened the door …. (quiet).

Language focus 2 Past simple vs. continuous

1 Look at the examples from the listening on page 34. Then complete rules 1 and 2 with *past simple* or *past continuous*.

- Something strange **happened** to me today while I **was shopping**.
- When I got to the cake shop, four people **were waiting**.

We use:
the ¹…. to talk about activities in progress at a moment in the past.
the ²…. to talk about a short, finished action which happens in the middle of another activity.

➡ Grammar reference • page 102

Get it right!

Use *when*, not *while*, to talk about something that happens at a point in time.
~~While the phone rang.~~ ✗
When the phone rang. ✓

2 Write sentences in past simple and continuous with *when* or *while* and the words below.
1 I / watch / TV / best friend / call
2 My dad / drive / home from work / car / suddenly / stop
3 I / walk / home from school / start / rain
4 I / see / you / you / wait / at the bus stop
5 My mum / read / a book / my brother / come home

3 Write questions with the past continuous or past simple form of the verb in brackets.
1  (rain) when you woke up this morning?
2 …. your phone …. (ring) while you were having breakfast?
3 …. anything strange …. (happen) while you were going to school?
4 When you got to school, …. your friends …. (play) football?
5 When you went into the classroom, …. your teacher …. (write) on the board?
6 While you were listening to the teacher, …. you …. (look) out of the window?

Your turn

4 Work with a partner. Ask and answer the questions in Exercise 3. Did you have the same kind of morning?

> Was it raining when you woke up this morning?

> No, it wasn't but I woke up very early. Was it raining when you woke up?

could(n't)

5 Complete the examples from the listening on page 34 with *could* or *couldn't* and the verb in brackets.

+ I ¹…. (play) it well when I was younger.
− I ²…. (not hear) her very well.

➡ Grammar reference • page 102

6 Which of the things in the box could you do when you were at primary school? Write sentences with *could* or *couldn't* and an adverb from page 34.

ride a bike   swim 25 metres
play a musical instrument   use a computer
speak two languages   sing
play your favourite sport

I could swim 25 metres quickly but I couldn't speak English well.

Your turn

7 Work with a partner. Ask and answer questions about the things in Exercise 6.

> Could you swim 25 metres when you were in primary school?

> Yes, I could swim 25 metres quickly.

Discover Culture

1 Look at the pictures and answer the questions.
  1 What is different about the two pictures?
  2 How do you think life in the two places is different?

2 ▶ 3.2 Watch the first part of the video (0.00–1.17) and check your answers to Exercise 1. What are the names of the two places?

Find out about a lost city under the water.

3.2 A story from under the sea

3 ▶ 3.2 Watch the second part and complete Kihachiro Aratake's story.

This is Kihachiro Aratake – he's a ¹…. He was diving near the ²…. of Yonaguni when he found something amazing. It looked like a small ³…. under the water. It had ⁴…., steps and tall towers. One stone had strange marks – was it ancient writing? Some ⁵…. think this structure is over 10,000 years old. They say it was once above the water.

4 Test your memory. Mark the sentences true (T) or false (F). Correct the false sentences.
  1 Yonaguni is very close to Japan.
  2 An old man is telling stories to some children.
  3 Some people are dancing.
  4 Kihachiro is with some friends on the boat.
  5 He swims down the 'streets' of the underwater city.
  6 There are lots of fish swimming around the ancient stones.

5  3.2 Watch the video again. Check your answers to Exercise 4 and choose the best summary for the video.
  1 Yonaguni is a secret place where people go on holiday.
  2 Yonaguni is a calm place where people have a lot of time to do what they like.
  3 Yonaguni is mysterious and we don't know much about its ancient stories.

Your turn

6 Work with a partner. Ask and answer the questions.
  1 What are the good things about living in a big capital city?
  2 What are the good things about living on a small island?
  3 Are there any mysterious places in your country like the underwater city? Where are they? What is their story?

Reading An article

1 Look at the map and the photo. Where is Easter Island? What can you see in the picture? Who do you think built the statues?

2 🔊 1.27 Read the article and match the questions with the paragraphs.
a Was life on the island always easy?
b Where is Easter Island?
c Who built the stone statues?
d Why is it called Easter Island?

3 Read the text again and order the events.
a There wasn't enough food.
b Explorers called the island Easter Island.
c People arrived on the island from Polynesia.
d The islanders built large stone statues.
e 111 people lived on the island.
f People started fighting each other.

Explore nouns with -er

4 Complete the table with -er nouns. The first three are in the article.

	noun with -er		noun with -er
explore	1 *explorer*	paint	5 ....
farm	2	build	6 ....
island	3	shop	7 ....
swim	4	photograph	8 ....

➡ Vocabulary bank • page 110

Your turn

5 Work in small groups. Ask and answer the questions.
1 Would you like to live on Easter Island? Why/Why not?
2 Why do you think people from Polynesia travelled to Easter Island?
3 How do you think the islanders moved the statues next to the sea?

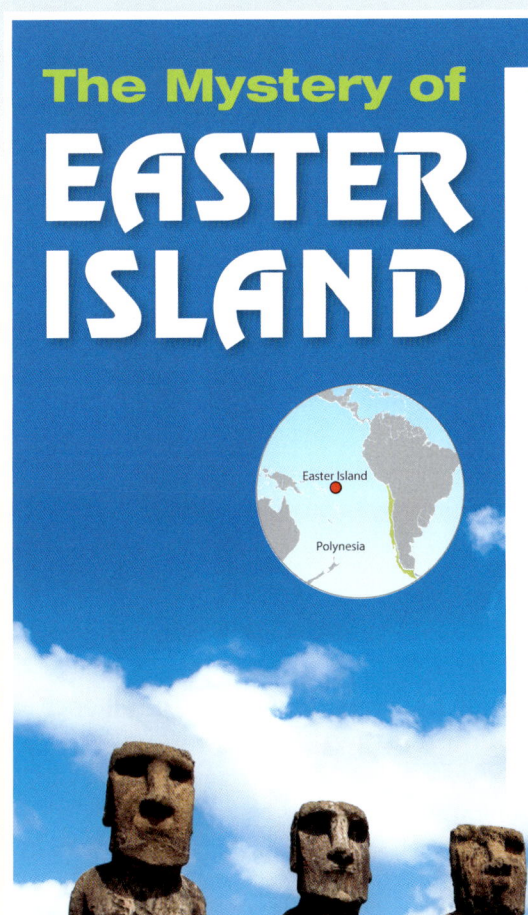

The Mystery of EASTER ISLAND

1 ....
When explorers landed on Easter Sunday, 5 April 1722, they called this island, Easter Island. They found some unusual things there; they weren't alone – people were living on the island and there were about 900 large stone statues.

2 ....
Easter Island is about 4,000km from any other country. Now you can fly there in about five hours from Chile but when the first people arrived from Polynesia between the years AD 300 and 1000, the only way to get there was a very long journey by boat.

3 ....
For thousands of years, life was easy for the people on Easter Island. At first, they were successful farmers and they also caught fish. At one time, around 12,000 people lived here. But at the start of the 17th century, the people were fighting each other because there wasn't enough food. In 1877, instead of over 10,000 people, there were only 111 left.

4 ....
When things were better, the islanders built the statues. Then they moved the statues so that they were next to the sea. All the statues had eyes so they could watch over the people on Easter Island.

FACT! *The statues are very heavy. Some weigh over 80,000 kgs. The islanders moved some of the statues 16 km to the sea.*

Speaking Telling someone your news

Real talk: What's an interesting or unusual thing that happened to you recently?

1 ▶ 3.3 Watch the teenagers in the video and put the sentences in the correct order.
a) I lost my cat.
b) I scored the winning goal.
c) There was some chocolate on everybody's desk.
d) My lunch wasn't there. *1*
e) We were wearing the same shirt.
f) The lock on my bike wasn't there.

2 What's an interesting or unusual thing that happened to *you* recently? Ask and answer with your partner.

3 🔊 1.28 Listen to Alice telling Lisa an interesting story. What did Alice win?

4 🔊 1.28 Complete the conversation with the useful language. Then, listen and check your answers.

Useful language

Really? What?
What did you say?
Something strange happened
How/That's weird!
What happened next?
What did you do?

Alice: ¹…. this morning!
Lisa: ²….
Alice: Well, I was walking into class when my phone rang.
Lisa: ³….
Alice: Well, I answered it and a woman I didn't know started speaking.
Lisa: ⁴….
Alice: She asked 'Is that Alice Bradman?' I said, 'yes'. And then she said, 'Alice, you're the winner in our photography competition.'
Lisa: Wow! ⁵….
Alice: I said 'Great! Thank you very much!'
Lisa: Cool! But Alice, you never take photos.
Alice: I know and I never enter competitions!
Lisa: Oh! ⁶…. ! What did you win?
Alice: A new digital camera!

5 Work with a partner. Practise the conversation in Exercise 4.

6 💬 Think of an interesting story. Use the useful language to ask and answer questions about your story with your partner.

7 💬 Change partners. Take turns to tell each other your interesting story.

> Something strange happened this morning
> Really? What?
> Well, I was…
> What did you do?

38

Writing A story

1 Look at the picture and read the story. Who is the man in the picture and what is he doing?

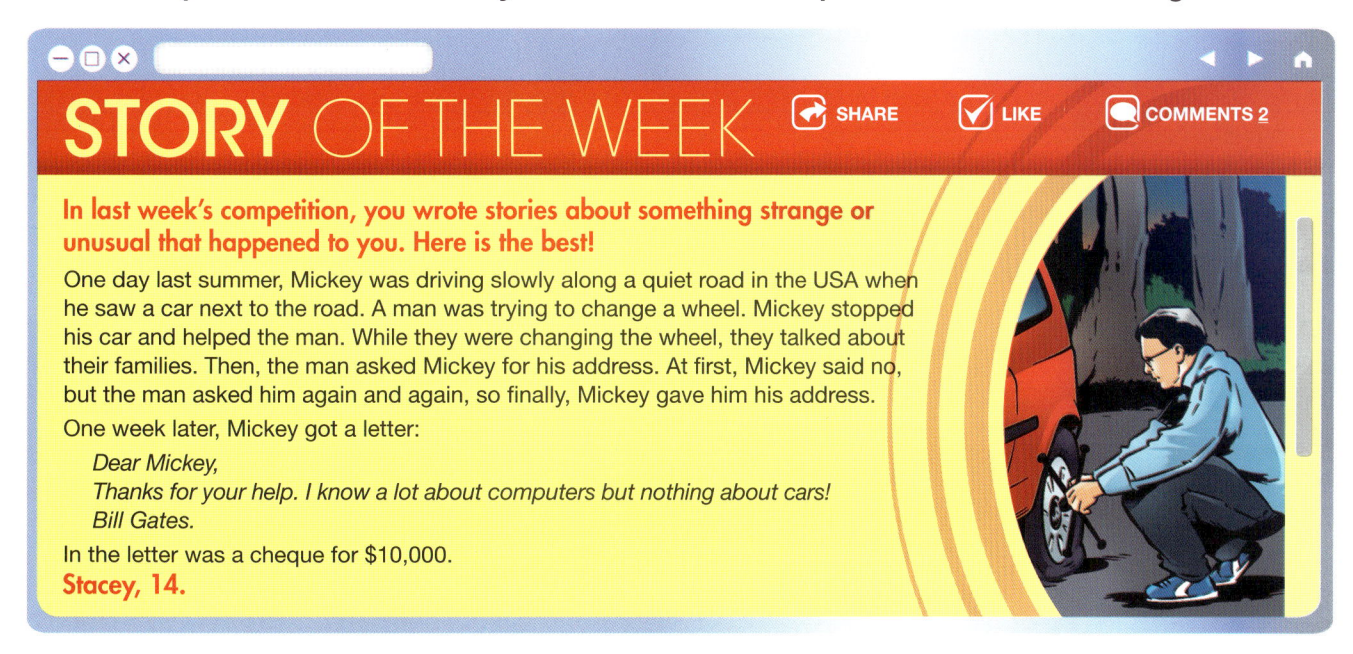

STORY OF THE WEEK

In last week's competition, you wrote stories about something strange or unusual that happened to you. Here is the best!

One day last summer, Mickey was driving slowly along a quiet road in the USA when he saw a car next to the road. A man was trying to change a wheel. Mickey stopped his car and helped the man. While they were changing the wheel, they talked about their families. Then, the man asked Mickey for his address. At first, Mickey said no, but the man asked him again and again, so finally, Mickey gave him his address.

One week later, Mickey got a letter:

Dear Mickey,
Thanks for your help. I know a lot about computers but nothing about cars!
Bill Gates.

In the letter was a cheque for $10,000.
Stacey, 14.

2 Answer the questions about the story.
1. When did the story happen?
2. Where did the story happen?
3. Who were the people in the story?
4. What happened in the beginning, in the middle and at the end of the story?

Useful language

Sequencing language 1
We use sequencing language to …
- start a story (*One day* last summer, …)
- order events (*At first,* Mickey said no.)
- finish a story (*Finally,* Mickey gave him his address.)

3 Find more examples of sequencing language in the text in Exercise 1.

4 Complete the paragraph with the words in the box.

Finally   first   ~~one~~   then   when   While

¹ *One* afternoon I was doing my homework quietly in my bedroom ² …. I heard a strange noise outside. At ³ …., I didn't want to go outside, but ⁴ …. I opened the door and went into the garden. There was a very small dog. ⁵ …. I was playing with the dog, my mum came home. She was laughing. Five minutes later, my dad and sister arrived. They were laughing too. ⁶ …., I understood. The dog was my birthday present!

Get Writing

PLAN

5 Make notes about something strange or unusual that happened to you. It can be true or invented. Use the questions in Exercise 2.

WRITE

6 Write your story. Use your notes from Exercise 5, and the language below.

One day/night last week/month/year…
He/she was …ing when …
Then, …
While he/she was …ing …
At first, … but …
So finally, …
Two days/weeks/months later …

CHECK

7 Can you say YES to these questions?
- Have you got sequencing language to show the order the events happened?
- Have you got the information from Exercise 5?
- Have you got the language from Exercise 6?

4 At home

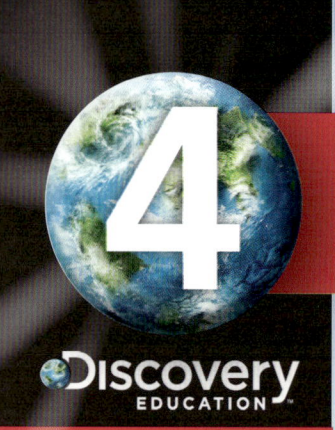

Discovery EDUCATION

In this unit …

Moving house **p43**

A cool life **p46**

Houses or flats? **p48**

CLIL The seventh wonder of the world **p119**

Vocabulary
- Things in the home
- Household appliances
- Expressions with *do*
- Verbs with *up* or *down*

Language focus
- Comparatives and superlatives
- *must / mustn't* and *should / shouldn't*

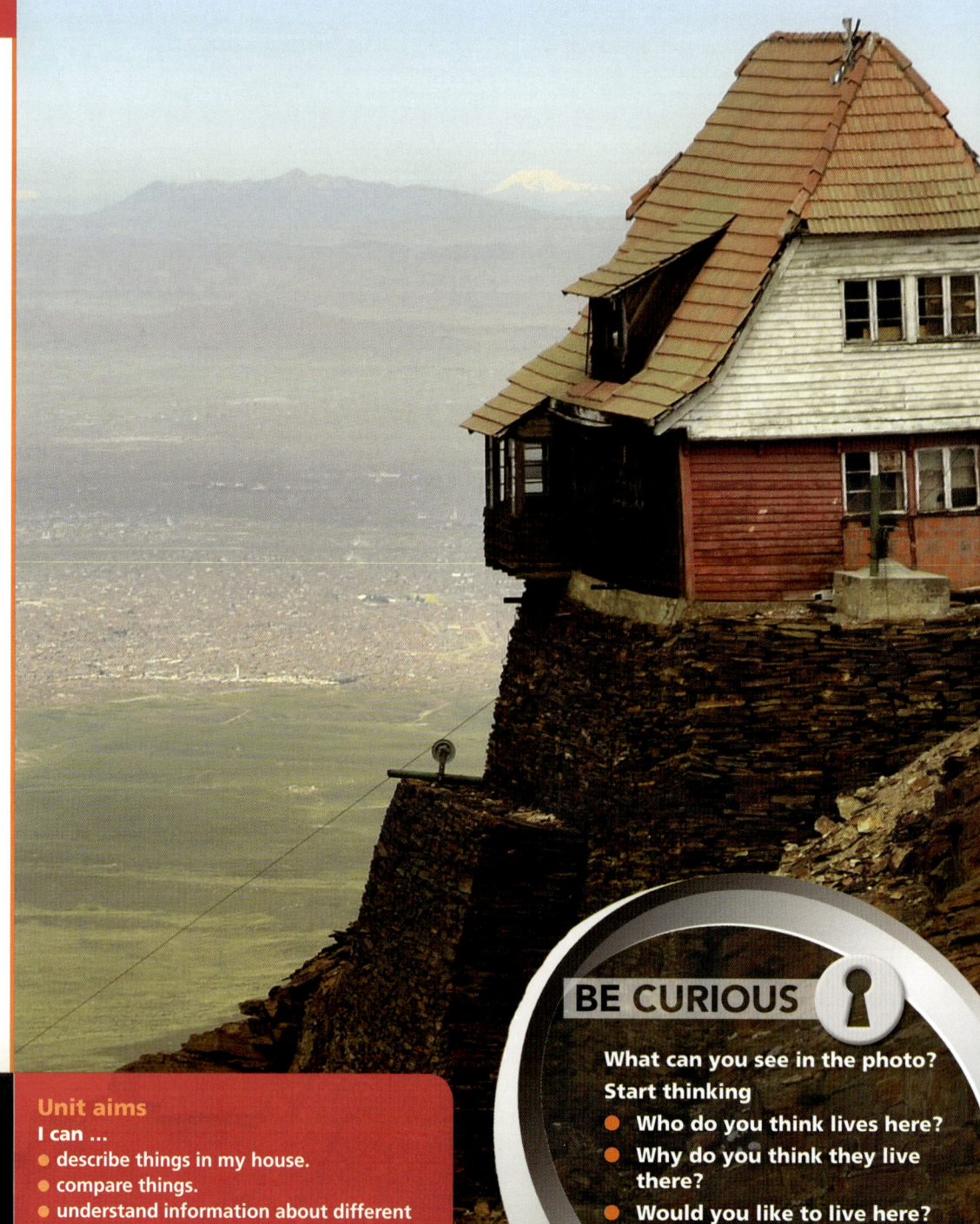

Unit aims
I can …
- describe things in my house.
- compare things.
- understand information about different places to stay or live.
- talk about things I need to do and things which are a good idea to do.
- ask for and offer help.
- write a description of my dream house.

BE CURIOUS

What can you see in the photo?
Start thinking
- Who do you think lives here?
- Why do you think they live there?
- Would you like to live here? Why/Why not?

Vocabulary Things in the home

1 🔊 **1.29** Match the pictures with the words in the box and name the other things in the rooms. Then listen, check and repeat.

> carpet   curtains   pillow   towel   mirror   wardrobe   cupboard   blanket   shelf   desk   sink

2 Look again at Exercise 1. Which …
1 two things can you put on your bed?
2 two things do you put things in?
3 two things do you put things on?
4 thing do you close at night and open in the morning?
5 thing can you see yourself in?
6 thing do we put on the floor?

Your turn

3 Draw a plan of your bedroom. Include some of the things in Exercise 1.

4 Describe your bedroom to your partner. Your partner listens and draws it. Then swap.

> In my bedroom, I've got a large bed in the middle of the room with two pillows and a green blanket.

➡ **Vocabulary bank** • page 111

Reading An online forum

1 Work with a partner. What's unusual about the hotels in the photos?

2 🔊 1.30 Read the online forum and check your ideas to Exercise 1. Then match the pictures to the posts (1–3).

3 Read the online forum again. Match the sentences with the hotels they describe.
1 This hotel isn't in Europe. *Hotel 2*
2 This hotel closes in the summer.
3 A family stayed at this hotel.
4 You can't use a hairdryer at this hotel.
5 The hotel is nearest to the sea.
6 The temperature in the hotel is below zero.

🔍 Explore expressions with *do*

4 Find two examples of *do* in the text. Which words follow them?

5 Make sentences about you and your family with *do* and the words in the box.

> housework   the washing   homework
> Maths   sports   the shopping

I did some housework on Saturday.

➡ **Vocabulary bank** • page 111

Your turn

6 Think of an idea for an unusual hotel. Write a short paragraph for the online forum. Talk about the things in the box.

> the place   the view   activities

We stayed in an unusual hotel. It was an old ship under the sea. My bedroom…

7 Compare your ideas in groups. Then choose your favourite.

THE MOST
Unusual Hotels
IN THE WORLD

There are many different hotels in the world; hotels for doing sports, city hotels or hotels for doing nothing. Last week, we asked you to tell us about the strangest hotels you know.

1 My parents stayed at the coldest hotel in the world – the Ice Hotel in Sweden. Open from December to April, it's the largest hotel made of snow and ice in the world. Their room was -5° C, but they said that the ice bed was more comfortable than their bed at home and the pillows were softer!
POSTED BY JACOB WILLIAMS 17:08   REPLY

2 When my cousin got married, she slept in the underwater room at a hotel on Pemba, one of the loveliest islands off the east coast of Africa. Every morning, they opened their curtains and saw the most beautiful fish in the world. They even swam with them!
POSTED BY LUCINDA THOMAS 15:59   REPLY

3 My family lives in the middle of Manchester. On holiday this year, we stayed at a treehouse hotel in a beautiful forest in Wales. It was much better than being in the city. Our bedrooms were high up in the trees. It was quieter and more relaxing and we did everything more slowly. But the worst thing? There wasn't any electricity so no TV!
POSTED BY NITA MEHTA 14:47   REPLY

FACT! Capsule hotels began in Japan. The very small rooms or 'capsules' are big enough for a bed and nothing else so guests share a bathroom in the hall. The good thing is that they are cheaper than many other hotels.

Language focus 1 Comparatives

1 Complete examples 1–4 from the text on page 42.

		Comparatives		Superlatives
short adjectives	soft	The pillows were ¹….	strange	Tell us about the ⁵…. hotels in the world.
long adjectives	comfortable	The ice bed was ²…. than their bed at home!	beautiful	… and saw the ⁶…. fish in the world …
irregular adjectives	good	It was much ³…. than being in the city.	bad	But the ⁷…. thing?
adverbs	slowly	We did everything ⁴….	quietly	I spoke **the most quietly**.

→ Grammar reference • page 103

→ Say it right! • page 96

2 Complete the sentences with the comparative form of the adjective or adverb in brackets.
1. London is ….*smaller*…. (small) than New York.
2. A holiday in the Amazon rainforest is …. (exciting) than a holiday in Paris.
3. I sleep …. (good) in my house than in a hotel.
4. My grandparents' house is …. (big) than my house.
5. I can study …. (easily) at school than at home.
6. My school canteen …. (noisy) than my classroom.

Superlatives

3 Complete examples 5–7 in the table above.

4 Write superlative sentences to complete the quiz. Then mark the sentences true (T) or false (F).

1. Russia / large / country in the world
2. Kilimanjaro / high / mountain in the world
3. Death Valley in California / hot / place in the world
4. The Atlantic / large / ocean in the world
5. The Vatican / small / country in the world
6. The cheetah / fast / animal in the world
7. The elephant / heavy / animal in the world

1 *Russia is the largest country in the world. T*

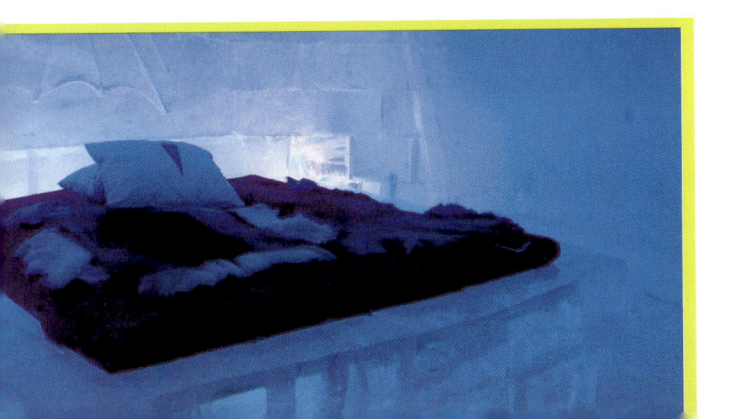

5 Choose the correct words.

Thousands of people visit Matmata in Tunisia every year. It's one of the ¹**more / most** popular places in this country because it's got some of the ²**stranger / strangest** and also some of the ³**older / oldest** homes in the world. Visitors can stay in a small underground hotel or in a ⁴**larger / largest** modern hotel, which is ⁵**more / most** expensive but less interesting. Why do so many people come here? Well, look at the photo ⁶**more / most** carefully. Do you know it? They made the film *Star Wars* here!

Your turn

6 Think about your dream hotel room. Make some notes. Then draw a picture.

7 Work with a partner. Describe and compare the pictures of your hotel rooms. Which is best?

> My hotel room has got big windows. What about yours?

Learn about Joey and his Yukon log cabin.
- Why did Joey move out of his father's house?
- What was the problem with the log cabin?
- What did Joey decide to do with the cabin?

4.1 Moving house

Listening An interview

1 Theo is from the USA. Look at the photos. Where does he live? Do you think his life is easy?

2 🔊 1.33 Listen to the interview with Theo. Check your ideas to Exercise 1.

3 🔊 1.33 Listen again. Answer the questions.
   1 Where does Theo go to school?
   2 What jobs does Theo do?
   3 What does Theo's dad do in the circus?
   4 When do they have circus training?
   5 What does he say about his life at the end of the interview?

Vocabulary Household appliances

4 🔊 1.34 Match the pictures with the words in the box. Then listen check and repeat.

> washing machine   fridge   heater   lamp
> cooker   hairdryer   freezer   iron   dishwasher

Your turn

5 Write your answers to the questions.
   1 How often do you use the things in Exercise 4?
   2 What housework do you usually do?
   3 Do you think it's important for children to help their parents at home?

   I use the dishwasher every day and I sometimes use the …

6 Work with a partner. Ask and answer the questions in Exercise 5. Who helps more at home?

   How often do you use the dishwasher?

   I use it every day. What about you?

➡ Vocabulary bank • page 111

Language focus 2 *must/mustn't, should/shouldn't*

1 Complete the examples from the listening on page 44.

+	I ¹.... study a lot.
−	We ².... miss a class.

2 Look at the sentences in Exercise 1. Then complete the rules with *must* or *mustn't*.

We use ¹.... to say you need to do something.
We use ².... to say you can't do something.

➔ Grammar reference • page 103

3 Choose the correct words.
1 You **must / mustn't** have a passport to go to the USA.
2 You **must / mustn't** go to school.
3 You **must / mustn't** use your mobile when you're driving.
4 You **must / mustn't** wear a seat belt in a car.
5 You **must / mustn't** leave a shop without paying.
6 You **must / mustn't** buy a ticket on a bus or train.

4 Complete the examples from the listening on page 44.

+	The teacher says I ¹.... work harder.
−	Some people say we ².... play with them.

5 Look at the sentences in Exercise 4. Then complete the rules with *should* or *shouldn't*.

We use ¹.... to say something is a good idea.
We use ².... to say something isn't a good idea.

➔ Grammar reference • page 103

6 Complete the sentences with *should* or *shouldn't* and the verb in brackets.
1 You ..*shouldn't forget*.. (forget) your parents' birthday.
2 You .... (put) another blanket on your bed, if you're cold.
3 You .... (visit) my city. It's fantastic!
4 You .... (swim) in the sea today. It's dangerous.
5 You .... (help) your parents with housework.
6 You .... (do) more exercise if you want to get fit.
7 You .... (go) to bed late the day before an exam.

👁 Get it right!
Use the infinitive without *to* after ***must(n't)*** and ***should(n't)***:
You must **tidy** your room before dinner. ✓
~~You must to tidy ...~~ ✗
You shouldn't **watch** TV so late if you're tired. ✓
~~You shouldn't to watch ...~~ ✗

UNIT 4

7 Complete the sentences about the UK with *must, mustn't, should* or *shouldn't*.

IN THE UK ...

you ¹ _must_ be over 17 to drive a car.
you ².... buy a licence for your television.
you ³.... say 'please' and 'thank you' as much as you can.
you ⁴.... walk or sit on the grass in some parks.
you ⁵.... give your seat to old people on a crowded bus or train.
you ⁶.... take a present if someone invites you to their house.
you ⁷.... open an umbrella inside the house.
you ⁸.... call your teacher by his or her first name.

Your turn

8 Work with a partner. Write sentences with *must, mustn't, should* and *shouldn't* about the places in the box.

> my house   my school   my sports centre
> my town   the cinema

I must tidy my room before school. I must put my plate in the dishwasher. I should take off my shoes when I get home…

9 Work in small groups. Read your sentences from Exercise 8. Can the others guess the place?

> I must tidy my room before school. I must put my plate in the dishwasher. I should take off my shoes when I get home …

> Is it your house?

> Yes, it is.

45

Discover Culture

1 **Work with a partner. Look at the pictures. Ask and answer the questions.**
   1 Where do you think the people in Coober Pedy live?
   2 What do you think the weather is like there?

2 ▶ 4.2 **Watch the video and check your answers to Exercise 1.**

3 **Test your memory. Which of the things below can you see in the video?**

   golf   football   cave   mines   swimming pool   beach   trucks
   diggers   precious stones   cactus   bedroom   factory

Find out about living in Coober Pedy.

Discovery EDUCATION
4.2 A cool life

4 ▶ 4.2 **Watch the video again. Check your answers to Exercise 3 and complete the sentences with up to three words.**
   1 In summer, the temperature is between 35 °C and *45 °C*.
   2 Candice White and her husband live in an ..... .
   3 Inside the house, the temperature can be ..... .
   4 The population of Coober Pedy is only ..... .
   5 Most people came to Coober Pedy to look for ..... .
   6 So, everybody lives and works ..... .

5 **Test your memory. Mark the sentences true (*T*) or false (*F*). Correct the false ones.**
   1 Opals are black.
   2 People wear lights on their heads to play golf.
   3 People wear lights on their heads in the mines.
   4 The golf ball is blue.
   5 The golf course is in the middle of the desert.

Your turn

6 **Compare living in your town in winter and in summer. Write sentences with the words in the box or your own ideas.**

   my house   clothes   sports
   food & drink   free time

   In winter, I've got more blankets on my bed.
   In summer, I use a thinner blanket.

7 **Work with a partner. Compare your sentences. Then decide if you prefer living in your town in the winter or in the summer.**

   In the winter, I've got more blankets on my bed. What about you?

   Me too and I wear warmer clothes and gloves.

Reading A blog

1 Look at the map and pictures. Where is Barrow? What do you think the weather is like there?

2 🔊 1.35 Read John's blog. Check your ideas to Exercise 1.

3 Read the blog again and choose the correct answer.
1. Barrow is further north than **Greenland / Russia / any other town in the USA**.
2. In winter, the temperature's usually **higher than 0 °C / lower than 0 °C / 0 °C**.
3. In June, in Barrow it's **light / dark / rainy**.
4. John would like to **move somewhere warmer / stay in Barrow / change school**.
5. Nalukataq is **John's school / the spring / a festival**.

Explore verbs with *up* or *down*

4 Look at the blog again. Find two verbs with *up* or *down*. What do they mean?

5 Complete the sentences with the verb in brackets and *up* or *down*.
1. The sun didn't ..*come up*.. until 7.30 this morning. (come)
2. If you know the answer, you should …. your hand. (put)
3. I'm tired. I want to …. on my bed. (lie)
4. Visitors often …. that hill because they can see the whole city from the top. (go)
5. Why are you sitting on top of the wardrobe? …. now! It's dangerous. (come)

➡ **Vocabulary bank** • page 111

Your turn

6 What are the best and worst things about living in your town? Write sentences with the words in the box or your own ideas.

> weather   people   food and drink   free-time activities   noise

One of the best things is the weather. It's warm and sunny in the summer.

7 Work in small groups. Would you prefer to live in your town or somewhere else? Use your ideas from Exercise 6.

Living in Barrow, Alaska

I'm John, from Barrow in Alaska, which is the most northern town in the USA. So what's it like living here? Well, in November, the sun goes down and it doesn't come up again until January. That means it's dark for 65 days. Of course, these are the coldest months of the year, even the highest temperature is below zero! It's also the most boring time of the year, we can't go out without our parents because it's too dark. Summer is better. In May, the sun stays up so there's no night for 85 days.

Why don't we move somewhere warmer? We love living here. I know everyone in the town, I love the school and we've got some amazing traditions and festivals. The best is Nalukataq in the spring when the fishermen return to our town with whale meat. Then, we make a special blanket. It's huge. A dancer stands in the middle of the blanket and we throw him or her into the air. When the dancer is in the air, they throw sweets to the children. It's fantastic – you should come and join us next year!

FACT! *The coldest inhabited place on Earth is Oymyakon in North East Russia. On 6 February 1933, it was –67.7 °C. That's freezing!*

Speaking Asking for and offering help

Real talk: Which do you prefer – houses or flats?

1 ▶ **4.3** Watch the teenagers in the video. Do they prefer flats (*F*), houses (*H*) or both (*B*)? Why?
a) Speaker 1   *H   bigger, more space*
b) Speaker 2
c) Speaker 3
d) Speaker 4
e) Speaker 5
f) Speaker 6

2 🗨 Work with your partner. Which do *you* prefer – houses or flats?

3 🔊 **1.36** Listen to Josh and his dad talking about housework. Which jobs does Josh agree to do?

4 🔊 **1.36** Complete the conversation with the useful language. Then listen and check your answers.

Useful language

Can you give me a hand?
I'll do it.
Can you do me a favour?

Yes, of course.
Shall I …?
I'll give you a hand.

Dad: Josh, dinner's nearly ready! ¹….
Josh: Yes. ²…. **lay the table**?
Dad: Thanks! ³…. Could you **take the dog for a walk** after dinner as well?
Josh: Sorry, Dad, I can't! **I've got a lot of homework to do.**
Dad: You always say that!
Josh: It's true! Anyway, it's **Hayley's** turn. Shall I ask her?
Dad: That's OK. ⁴….
Josh: OK. After dinner ⁵…. to **put the plates in the dishwasher**, but then I need to finish **an essay**.
Dad: OK. And can you go and tell **Hayley** it's dinnertime, please?
Josh: ⁶….

5 🗨 Work with a partner. Practise the conversation in Exercise 4.

6 🗨 Work with a partner. Change the words in bold in the conversation in Exercise 4. Use the ideas below or your own. Then practise the conversation.

do the washing   clean the microwave
tidy your room   wash up

Writing A description of a house

1 Look at the picture and read Kevin's description of his dream house. Would you like to live there?

> My dream home is a large modern house in the city centre. It's got two floors and a lift. Downstairs there's a living room with the biggest TV in the world. There's also a swimming pool and a tennis court.
>
> My bedroom's upstairs with its own bathroom. There's a jacuzzi in the bathroom and a huge brown bed in the middle of the bedroom with lots of pillows. Next to it, there's a machine for making fresh juice in the morning. There's a large window above my bed so I can see the whole city from here when the curtains are open. You should come and visit me soon!

2 Read Kevin's description again and answer the questions.
1. Is Kevin's dream home a flat or a house?
2. Where is it?
3. Where's Kevin's bedroom? What's it like?
4. What can Kevin do in his bedroom?

3 Look at the Useful language box. Find examples of adjectives in Kevin's description.

Useful language

Order of adjectives

When we use two or more adjectives together, we use this order:
- I've got a **brilliant new** computer.
- My mum bought me a **big red** towel for the beach.
- There's an **amazing purple** picture on the wall.

4 Complete the table with the words in the box.

> small   old   green and yellow   beautiful

Opinion	Fact			Noun
	Size	Age	Colour	
fantastic	large	new	blue	blanket
1	2	3	4	towel

5 Rewrite the sentences with the adjectives in brackets.
1. I've got a wardrobe. (old, large) *I've got a large old wardrobe.*
2. I'm sitting in my kitchen. (white, modern)
3. My grandparents have got a sofa in their living room. (red, comfortable)
4. We've got a fridge. (huge, silver)
5. There was a carpet on the floor. (red and black, strange)
6. I'd like to buy a laptop. (smaller, more modern)

Get Writing

PLAN

6 Make notes about your dream home. Use the questions in Exercise 2.

WRITE

7 Write a description of your dream home. Use your notes from Exercise 6, and the language below.

My dream home is …
It's got … and ….
Downstairs there's a … with …
There's also a …
Next to it, there's a …
You should come and visit me soon.

CHECK

8 Can you say YES to these questions?
- Have you got adjectives to describe the things in your home?
- Have you got the information from Exercise 6?
- Have you got the language from Exercise 7?

3-4 Review

Vocabulary

1 Match the sentence halves.
1. The thief climbed …
2. He jumped …
3. The police officer chased …
4. The police officer didn't …
5. The thief hid …
6. The thief threw …

a behind a tree.
b a tree.
c his bag into the river.
d into the garden.
e the thief for 2 km.
f catch the thief.

2 Complete the sentences with the adverbial form of the words in the box.

> happy   careful   easy   quick   quiet   slow

1. It's getting late. Please finish your work …. .
2. Please talk …. in the library.
3. The exam wasn't difficult. I passed it …. .
4. We're really late! You're walking very …. .
5. Your little brother isn't sad. He's …. eating an ice cream over there.
6. Those books are very old! Please look at them …. .

3 Read the descriptions of some things in the home. What is the word?
1. You put your clothes in this. w _ _ _ _ _ _ _
2. People use this to look at themselves. m _ _ _ _ _
3. This is something you put on your bed to feel warmer. b _ _ _ _ _ _
4. Students sit at this type of table to study. d _ _ _
5. You need this to dry yourself after a shower. t _ _ _ _
6. People wash dirty things in this. s _ _ _

4 Match the household appliances with the pictures.

> freezer   hairdryer   washing machine
> cooker   dishwasher

Explore vocabulary

5 Choose the correct answers.
1. I wanted to ask a question so I put **up / off** my hand.
2. My sister couldn't find her keys so I helped her look **for / at** them.
3. I was feeling ill so I went to lie **on / down**.
4. Your brother looks **for / like** a rock star with his long hair.
5. Could you look **after / up** my dog while I buy some milk?

6 Complete the sentences with the name of the person. Look at the words in bold to help you.
1. My brother takes a lot of **photographs**. He's an amazing *photographer* .
2. We visited the **island** of Malta last summer. The …. were very friendly.
3. My friend Julia **swims** very quickly. She's a champion …. .
4. My dad **builds** houses all week. He works as a …. .
5. My cousins live on a **farm** because their dad is a …. .
6. Marco Polo **explored** China. He was a famous …. .

7 Complete the sentences with *do* and the words in the box.

> homework   the shopping   Maths
> housework   sports   the washing

1. Can you buy some biscuits when you …. , please?
2. I sometimes …. at home. I tidy my bedroom and I empty the bins.
3. I have no clean clothes. I need to …. .
4. On Monday morning at school, we …. , and then Geography and English.
5. At school, we …. a lot of …. . My favourite one is tennis.
6. I often …. my …. in the library because it's very quiet there.

50

Language focus

1 Complete the questions and answers with the past continuous. Use the information in the table.

yesterday	Maria	Robert
10 am	play tennis	swim
12 noon	study with Robert	study with Maria

1 **A:** What ¹.... Maria .... at 10 am yesterday?
   B: She ².... tennis.
2 **A:** ³.... Robert .... tennis at 10 am yesterday?
   B: ⁴...., he .... He ⁵.... .
3 **A:** What ⁶.... Maria and Robert .... at 12 noon?
   B: They ⁷.... .

2 Write sentences using the past simple and past continuous.

1 He / answer / the phone / while / he / eat
   He answered the phone while he was eating.
2 We / have / a picnic / when / it / start to rain
3 Tara / break / her glasses / while / she / play tennis
4 I / read / a magazine / when / the window / break
5 The film / start / while / they / buy / tickets

3 Write sentences with *could/couldn't*.

	six years old	seven years old	ten years old
Marta	(1) count in English (✗)	(3) ride a skateboard (✓)	(5) play the violin (✓)
Sam	(2) swim ten metres (✓)	(4) use a computer (✗)	(6) make a cake (✗)

1 *Marta couldn't count in English when she was six.*

4 Write sentences with *be* and the comparative form of the adjectives.

1 Our new house / big / our old house
2 This small hotel / comfortable / a large hotel
3 These laptops / good / desktop computers
4 My class / noisy / your class
5 Your friends / interesting / my friends

5 Complete the sentences with the superlative form of the adjectives in brackets.

1 Burj Khalifa in Dubai is .... (tall) building in the world.
2 Mawsynram in India is .... (wet) place in the world.
3 Kilauea in Hawaii is .... (active) volcano in the world.
4 The cheetah is .... (fast) animal in the world.
5 Commonwealth Bay in Antarctica is .... (windy) place in the world.

6 Look at the sign. Then choose the correct answers.

Computer room rules	
No food!	Please talk quietly.
No computer games!	Please ask for help.
Don't use printers!	

1 You **mustn't** / **should** bring food into the room.
2 You **mustn't** / **shouldn't** play computer games.
3 You **should** / **shouldn't** talk loudly to your friends.
4 You **must** / **should** ask for help.
5 You **mustn't** / **shouldn't** use the printers.

Language builder

7 Choose the correct answers.

Kara: I ¹.... at my new school ².... week.
Jenny: How is it? Is it the ³.... school in the city?
Kara: I'm not sure about that but it's ⁴.... my house so now I've got ⁵.... for breakfast.
Jenny: Cool! ⁶.... you make friends on the first day?
Kara: Yes, of course. I also learned the rules. We mustn't ⁷.... inside and we ⁸.... switch off our mobile phones.

1	a start	b started
2	a past	b last
3	a better	b best
4	a near	b nearer
5	a enough time	b time enough
6	a Was	b Did
7	a run	b to run
8	a mustn't	b must

Speaking

8 Complete the conversations with the words in the box.

> How   Can you give me   Yes, of course   Shall I
> Something strange happened   What?

Liz: ¹.... this morning.
Pete: Really? ².... ?
Liz: A family of mice fell down our chimney and got into the living room!
Pete: ³.... weird!

Luke: These bags are heavy. ⁴.... a hand?
Jenny: ⁵.... . ⁶.... take the green bag?
Luke: Thanks.

5 Visions of the future

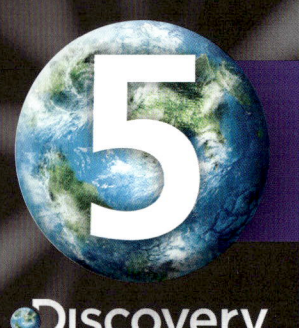

Discovery EDUCATION

In this unit ...

- Pizza problems p55 
- Learning to share p58 
- Mobile phones p60 
- Who's real? p120

Vocabulary
- Computer words
- Technology verbs + prepositions
- Suffixes -*ful* and -*less*
- Phrasal verbs 1

Language focus
- *will/won't, may/might*
- First conditional

Unit aims
I can ...
- talk about computers and technology.
- make predictions about the future.
- understand information about what the future will be like.
- talk about what will happen if I do something.
- ask for and give instructions.
- write an opinion essay.

BE CURIOUS

What can you see in the photo?
Start thinking
- Will we live in cities like these in the future?
- How will school be different?
- What will we do in our free time?

Vocabulary Computer words

1 🔊 **2.01** Match the pictures with the words in the box. Then listen check and repeat.

> keyboard   laptop   memory stick   mouse   printer
> tablet   touchscreen   microchip   smartphone

2 Choose the correct words.
1. You can write an email with **a mouse / a keyboard**.
2. You can save your work on **a memory stick / a printer**.
3. **A microchip / a tablet** has usually got a touchscreen.
4. You can carry **a smartphone / a laptop** easily in one hand.
5. A touchscreen computer doesn't need **a mouse / a microchip**.
6. People often take their **printer / laptop** on holiday.

Your turn

3 Write answers to the questions.
1. How often do you use a computer? What do you use it for?
2. Which things in Exercise 1 do you use at home? What do you use them for?
3. Which things in Exercise 1 do you use at school? What do you use them for?

4 Ask and answer the questions in Exercise 3 with a partner. Listen and make notes.

➡ **Vocabulary bank** • page 112

COMPUTERS
PAST, PRESENT AND FUTURE

Sixty-five years ago, scientists called the first computer 'Baby'. But it was huge. It needed a whole room to itself! A team of people wrote three Maths problems and then waited 52 minutes for Baby to find the answer to just one of them. At the time, this was amazing.

Computers are now both much smaller, don't forget your smartphone is a mini computer, and also more powerful. There is more power in a smartphone than in all the computers on Apollo 11, the first spacecraft on the moon! What's more, with new touchscreen technology, soon we won't need extra things like a keyboard or a mouse.

So, how will computers change in the future? A computer's 'brain' is in its chip and in the future scientists will be able to save much more information on this. So, computers will be smaller and even more powerful and they may even think like humans. In the future, we may not need to tell computers what to do because they might decide for themselves.

FACT! Need a new hip, knee or face? Doctors can now use 3D printers to make some parts of the body.

Reading A magazine article

1 Look at the photos. How was the first computer different from modern computers?

2 🔊 2.02 Read the article and check your ideas to Exercise 1.

3 Read the text again. Choose the correct answers.
  1 The first computer was … .
     a very small   b very big   c a baby
  2 Baby found the answer to … in 52 minutes.
     a three Maths problems   b an exam question
     c one Maths problem
  3 The computers on Apollo 11 were … a smartphone.
     a more powerful than   b less powerful than
     c as powerful as
  4 In the next few years we won't need … .
     a keyboards   b smartphones
     c touchscreens

Explore suffixes -ful and -less

4 Look at the article again. What do we add to the noun *power* to make an adjective? What do you think we add to make the negative form?

5 Complete the sentences with the correct adjective form (*-ful* or *-less*) of the noun in brackets.
  1 Jennifer Lawrence is a very good actor and she's ...*beautiful*... .   (beauty)
  2 We never use that old computer, it's slow and … .   (use)
  3 I love my touchscreen laptop. It's … .   (wonder)
  4 I fell over and hurt my knee yesterday. It's very … now.   (pain)
  5 My brother makes a lot of mistakes. He's very … .   (care)
  6 I think I'll pass the test. I'm … .   (hope)

➡ **Vocabulary bank** • page 112

Your turn

6 Write down three things you'd like your computer to do in the future.
I'd like my computer to clean my room.

7 Compare your lists from Exercise 6. Work with a partner. Who has the best idea?

Language focus 1 *will/won't, may/might*

1 Complete the examples from the text on page 54.

+	Computers ¹.... be smaller. They ².... even think like humans. They ³.... decide for themselves.
−	We ⁴.... need extra things like a keyboard. We ⁵.... need to tell computers what to do. We **might not** need a mouse.
?	How ⁶.... computers change in the future? **Will** computers be more powerful?

➡ Grammar reference • page 104

2 Which two words can you use when you are sure about the future?

> will   won't   may   might

➡ Say it right! • page 96

> 👁 **Get it right!**
> After *will* or *won't*, we use the infinitive without *to*.
> I **will see** Andy ✓
> ~~I will to see Andy~~ ✗

3 In 1900, an American engineer made these predictions about the world. Complete the sentences with *will* or *won't* and the verbs in the box.

> ~~send~~   call   not wait   live   not cook   be   eat   buy

1 People ....*will send*.... photos to their friends all over the world.
2 Americans .... 5 cm taller.
3 A husband at work in Chicago .... his wife at home in New York.
4 We .... our own meals. We .... them in shops.
5 Between 300 and 500 million people .... in the USA.
6 We .... until summer to eat tomatoes. We .... them in the winter too.

4 Which of the predictions in Exercise 3 are true now?

5 Write sentences about the year 2040 with *will, won't, may, might*. Use your opinion.
1 We / have Wi-Fi connections in our clothes.
We won't have Wi-Fi connections in our clothes. We'll have them on our heads!
2 Cars / need a human driver.
3 People / live to be 120 years old.
4 Robots / cook our meals.
5 There / be pens and pencils.
6 We / use our mobiles to turn on everything.
7 I / work in an office. I / work at home.
8 There / be shops and town centres.

Your turn

6 Make predictions about your future with *will, won't, may* or *might*. Write sentences with the things in the box or use your own ideas.

> your friends   your town   your studies
> your job   your family   your house

I'll go to university to study Medicine and then I might work as a doctor.

7 Work with a partner. Compare your sentences from Exercise 6. Choose the three best predictions and tell the class.

> We'll have the same friends as now but we may also make some new friends.

Learn about how to use technology to get a takeaway pizza.
● How do they do it?
● What's good and bad about their idea?
● Can you think of a better idea?

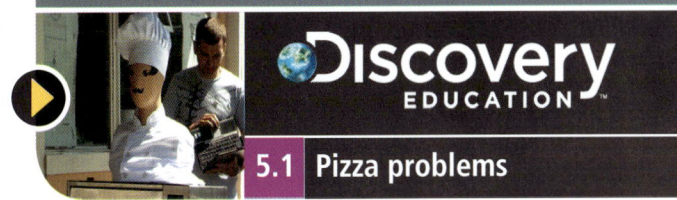

5.1 Pizza problems

Listening An interview

1 Look at the photo. What do you think it is?

2 🔊 2.05 Listen to Judy interviewing Paul. Check your ideas to Exercise 1.

3 🔊 2.05 Listen again. Mark the sentences true (*T*) or false (*F*). Correct the false sentences.
   1 Judy thinks it's very small for a computer.
   2 This computer has got a big screen.
   3 The computer is expensive and difficult to use.
   4 Pupils in the UK are using this computer in their lessons.
   5 'Code' is what people use to program computers.
   6 Paul made a music program yesterday with the computer.

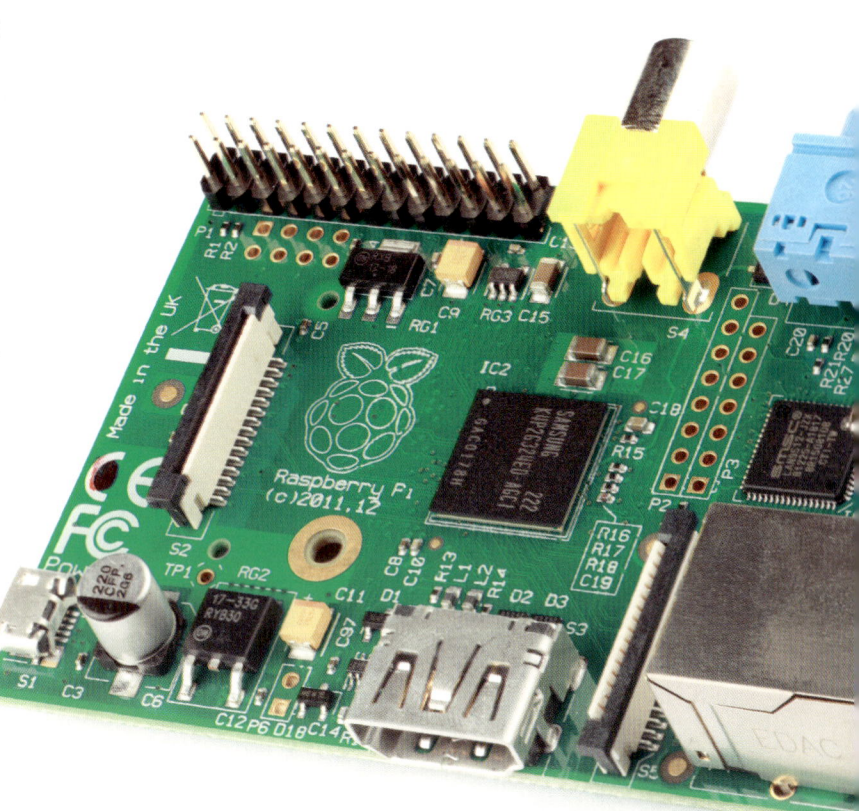

Vocabulary Technology verbs + prepositions

4 🔊 2.06 Match the pictures with the actions. Then listen, check and repeat.
   1 Scroll down the webpage.
   2 Sign into your account.
   3 Turn on the laptop.
   4 Click on the icon.
   5 Turn up the volume.
   6 Shut down the computer.
   7 Turn down the volume.
   8 Log onto your computer.

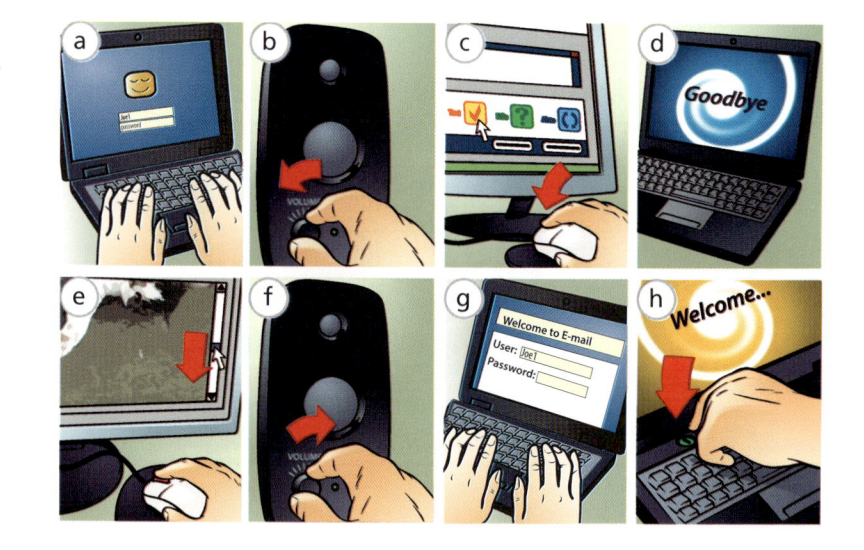

Your turn

5 Write sentences to tell your partner how to do the things below on a computer. Use the vocabulary in Exercise 4.

   > watch a video   read a blog
   > listen to music   write an email

   First, turn on the laptop ... , then ...

6 Work with a partner. Student A: Tell your partner how to do the things in Exercise 5. Student B: Listen and write down the vocabulary from Exercise 4 in the order your partner says it. Then swap.

   ➡ Vocabulary bank • page 112

Language focus 2 First conditional

1 Complete the examples from the listening on page 56. Then answer the question below.

action/situation	result
If we ¹.... it on here, If you ².... it in like this,	you'll see it's a computer. you won't.

result	action/situation
I ³.... **show** you how the computer works	if you've **got** time.
Questions	
How ⁴.... I .... it	if it **hasn't got** a mouse?

5 Do *if* and *will* go in the same part of the sentence?

→ Grammar reference • page 104

2 Choose the correct words.
1. If my brother **learns / will learn** to write code, he **gets / will get** a job as a computer programmer.
2. If my parents **get / will get** a new computer, I **don't buy / won't buy** a tablet.
3. The TV **doesn't work / won't work** if you **don't plug / won't plug** it in.
4. I **buy / will buy** a new mobile if I **get / will get** enough money for my birthday.
5. **Will we watch / Do you watch** a film if we **finish / will finish** early?
6. If it **rains / will rain** all weekend, we **go / will go** to the cinema.
7. If you **decide / will decide** to play football, **do you call / will you call** me?

3 Look at the picture and read the text. How will the boy become famous?

4 🔊 2.07 Complete the text in Exercise 3 with the correct form of the verbs in brackets. Then listen and check.

Your turn

5 Complete the first conditional sentences below so they are true for you.
1. If I have a video channel one day, *I'll post a funny video*.
2. If my favourite team wins the league, ...
3. If I don't go out this weekend, ...
4. If I pass all my exams, ...
5. If my phone breaks, ...
6. If my parents give me some pocket money, ...
7. If it rains all weekend, ...

6 Work with a partner. Ask and answer questions about your sentences in Exercise 5.

> What will you do if you have a video channel one day?

> I'll post funny videos.

SO MANY IFS!

If I ¹.... (pass) my exams this term, my parents ².... (buy) me a new computer. If I ³.... (get) a new computer, I ⁴.... (start) my own YouTube channel. I ⁵.... (post) videos of my dog if I ⁶.... (get) my own channel. Everybody ⁷.... (be) amazed if they ⁸.... (see) her playing football on the beach! If one million people ⁹.... (like) my channel, I ¹⁰.... (be) famous!

Discover Culture

1 Work with a partner. Match the pictures with the words in the box.

> file sharing   cassettes   downloading   CDs   music streaming   records

2 Order the ways of listening to music from oldest to newest. Can you think of any other ways of listening to music?

Find out about Napster.

Discovery EDUCATION

5.2 Learning to share

3 Look at the pictures and the title of the video. What do you think Napster is?

4 ▶ 5.2 Watch the video and check your answer to Exercise 3.

5 Test your memory. Put events a–f in the same order as the video.
   a Record companies and musicians weren't happy.
   b The lawyers stopped Napster but people continue to share files.
   c People bought CDs and listened to them on CD players.
   d Shawn Fanning wrote a computer program called Napster.
   e Young people began to download music from the Internet.
   f Napster became very popular and people stopped going to music shops.

6 ▶ 5.2 Watch the video again and check your answers to Exercise 5.

Your turn

7 Work in small groups. Ask and answer the questions.
   1 Do you think closing down Napster was a good decision? Why/Why not?
   2 Do you ever buy CDs, or do you know anybody who buys them?
   3 Do you download music? How often? From where?
   4 Do you share music with your friends? How do you do it?
   5 Do you listen to streamed music online? If so, how do you do this?

8 Write sentences about your group's answers with *some of us*, *none of us* and *all of us*.

None of us buy CDs. All of us download music. Some of us share music with …

UNIT 5

Reading A blog

1. Look at the map and the photos. Where does Riley Stanton live? Where do you think he goes to school?

2. 🔊 **2.08** Read Riley's blog about life on a farm and check your ideas to Exercise 1.

3. Read the blog again. Are the sentences 'Right' (*A*) or 'Wrong' (*B*)? If you cannot find the information choose 'Doesn't say' (*C*).
   1. Riley cleans the chicken house before breakfast. A B C
   2. Riley lives near his school. A B C
   3. Riley's teacher and classmates wait for him to come online. A B C
   4. Riley and his friends can look at the lesson again after class. A B C
   5. Riley understands the Science lesson. A B C
   6. Riley finishes his Maths homework before the class. A B C

🔍 Explore phrasal verbs 1

4. Find *get up* and *sit down* in the blog. What do they mean?

5. Match the sentence beginnings with the sentence endings.
   1. On a school day, I get
   2. I go to my classroom and I sit
   3. I put
   4. When I arrive at school, I take
   5. When I get to school, I look

   a. for my friends.
   b. up at 7 am.
   c. off my coat.
   d. on my shoes and then my coat.
   e. down at my desk.

➡ **Vocabulary bank** • page 112

Your turn

6. Work with a partner. Write down the good and bad things about using technology for learning.

7. Work in small groups. Compare your ideas and decide on the top three good and bad things about using technology for learning.

I CAN'T STUDY WITHOUT TECHNOLOGY!

Riley's farm

It's 6 am. I'm tired but it's time to get up. After cleaning the chicken house, I have breakfast. School starts at 8 am but my school is in my house, in a room we call the 'study room'. I can't go to school because it's 300 km away so I go to the School of the Air.

How does it work? Well, I sit down at my desk, turn on my laptop and wait for my teacher and my classmates to come online. Today it's Science. Our teacher uses the interactive whiteboard to explain some new ideas. She saves her work on the computer and shares this with us on the website. She then asks us some questions and we listen to everyone's answers. At the end of the lesson, we have to do a quiz on the website so she can see who doesn't understand. This lesson is only half an hour but it's tiring.

I quite enjoy studying at home. It's great to be near my family but I would like to meet my classmates. When I finish school, I would like to go to Alice Springs and study at the college there, then go to university. I want to be a pilot. But first, I've got to finish my Maths homework before the lesson today!

FACT! The School of the Air gives lessons to children in Australia who live in areas without schools. When it first started in 1951, the pupils listened to their lessons over the radio. Nowadays, they use the latest technology.

Speaking Asking for and giving instructions

Real talk: How important is your mobile to you?

1 ▶ 5.3 Watch the teenagers in the video. How important is their mobile to them? Write ✗ (not important), ✓ (quite important) or ✓✓ (very/really important).
- a) Speaker 1 ✗
- b) Speaker 2
- c) Speaker 3
- d) Speaker 4
- e) Speaker 5
- f) Speaker 6

2 How important is *your* mobile to *you*? Ask and answer with your partner.

3 🔊 2.09 Listen to Keira talking to her grandmother. What does her grandmother want to do?

4 🔊 2.09 Complete the conversation with the useful language. Then listen and check your answers.

Useful language

First, you need to …
You have to …
How do I … ?
Yes! That's it. Now …

How does it work?
Ok, here it is.
I see! Thanks!
and then …

Grandma:	Keira, can I borrow your phone to call Granddad?
Keira:	Yeah, sure but it's a smartphone.
Grandma:	Oh! ¹…. Where are the numbers?
Keira:	Well, it's got a touchscreen. ²…. press the round button at the bottom.
Grandma:	What? Like this?
Keira:	³…. swipe the bottom of the screen to unlock the phone.
Grandma:	Right! ⁴…. make a call?
Keira:	⁵…. touch the contacts icon, ⁶…. scroll down to Granddad's name.
Grandma:	⁷….
Keira:	If you tap Granddad's number, it'll ring him.
Grandma:	⁸….
Keira:	You're a fast learner!

5 Work with a partner. Practise the conversation in Exercise 4.

6 Work with a partner. Plan instructions for someone who can't use a smartphone. Choose one of the ideas below and the useful language from Exercise 4.

send a text   listen to music   check emails
surf the Internet   play a game

7 Change partners. Give instructions to your new partner.

> Can I borrow your phone to send a text?

> Yes, of course but it's a smartphone.

> Oh! How does it work?

Writing An opinion essay

UNIT 5

THIS WEEK'S COMPETITION!
Write an essay about the following subject: 'The future of music' If you're the winner, we'll give you a new tablet!

1 Read the competition advert and the '*Answer of the Month*'. What does Marcus think will happen to music in the future?

ANSWER OF THE MONTH!
THE FUTURE OF MUSIC

a In the future, technology will change many areas of our lives including how we buy and listen to music.

b **Firstly**, technology will change the way we buy music. Some people think that in a few years nobody will buy CDs and we will stream all our music from our smartphones. We might not even need a smartphone as our clothes might play music. **However**, others say that some people will always prefer to buy CDs from shops. For example, my dad loves talking to the shop assistants and bringing home new music.

c **Secondly**, technology will change which music we listen to. In the future, we won't choose what we want to listen to because our phones will know what we like and decide this for us.

d **In conclusion**, I'm sure that things will be different in the future but, in my opinion, some people will always want to buy CDs in a music shop and this will never change.

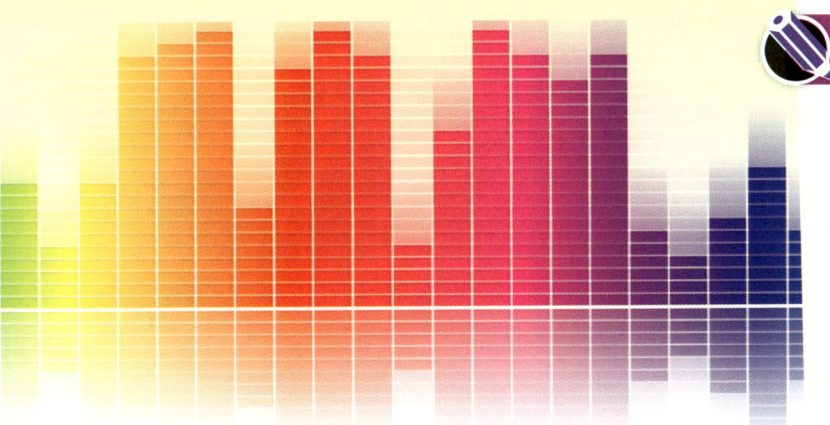

2 Read Marcus' answer again. In which paragraph (a–d) does he …
1 finish his essay by making a prediction about the future? *b*
2 give some people's opinion about the topic? ....
3 introduce a different opinion to the one before? ....
4 introduce the topic? ....

3 Match the words in **bold** in the text with 1–4 in the useful language.

Useful language

Sequencing language 2
Use sequencing language to …
- show a contrast ¹....
- introduce an opening point ²....
- summarise an opinion ³....
- introduce another point ⁴....

Get Writing

PLAN

4 Choose one of the essay titles below and make notes. Use the same order and information from Exercise 2.
- The future of school
- The future of mobile phones
- The future of computer games
- The future of TV

WRITE

5 Write your opinion essay. Use your notes from Exercise 4, and the language below.
In the future, …
Some people think that…
Others say that…
I'm sure that …
In my opinion, …

CHECK

6 Check your writing. Can you say YES to these questions?
- Have you got the information from Exercise 2?
- Have you got the language from Exercise 5?
- Have you got sequencing language?

6 Life choices

Discovery EDUCATION

In this unit ...

A school at home **p65**

Time for an adventure! **p68**

Future plans **p70**

CLIL Go green! **p121**

Vocabulary
- Life events
- Containers and materials
- Phrasal verbs 2
- Verbs with prepositions

Language focus
- *be going to*
- *be going to* and *will*
- Present continuous for future

Unit aims
I can ...
- talk about important life events.
- talk about my future plans and make predictions about my future.
- understand information about important events in our lives.
- make plans for next week with my friends.
- agree or disagree with someone's opinion.
- write a thank you email.

BE CURIOUS
What can you see in the photo?
Start thinking
- Where is the boy?
- What is he trying to decide?
- What big decisions will you need to make in your life?

Vocabulary Life events

1 🔊 **2.10** Match the pictures with the life events. Then listen, check and repeat.

> learn to drive   get married   start school   leave home   go to university
> have children   leave school   take a year out   be born   get a job

2 Write the events in Exercise 1 in the order they usually happen. Then compare your list with your partner.

Your turn

3 Which of the things in Exercise 1 would you like/not like to do?

4 Write sentences about the things you'd like to do and give more information.
I'd like to learn to drive when I'm eighteen and I'd like to go to university to study History.

5 Work with a partner. Ask and answer questions about your sentences from Exercise 4. Try to find something different.

> Would you like to learn to drive?

> Yes, I'd like to learn to drive when I'm eighteen. What about you?

➡ **Vocabulary bank** • page 113

Reading A magazine quiz

1 What do you want to be when you're older? Tell your partner.

2 🔊 2.11 Read the quiz and choose A, B or C.

3 Check the key on page 97. Do you agree with what the quiz says about you? Why/ Why not?

Explore phrasal verbs 2

4 Find three phrasal verbs in the quiz. What do they mean?

5 Complete the sentences with the words in the box.

> go out   grow up   try on   find out
> write down   get on/off

1 When I ...., I want to be a famous musician.
2 On Saturday afternoon, I often .... with my friends. We ride our bikes or go to the skate park.
3 To get to my house, ... the bus at the cinema and then .... opposite the park.
4 I always .... new English words in my notebook.
5 I never .... T-shirts before I buy them. I know my size.
6 If I want to know more about something, I use the Internet to .... .

➔ Vocabulary bank • page 113

Your turn

6 Rewrite the sentences in Exercise 5 about you so most of them are true and some of them are false.
When I grow up, I want to be a clown in a circus.

7 Work with a partner. Compare your sentences. Can you guess which are false?

> When I grow up, I want to be a clown in a circus.

> That's not true! You want to be a doctor.

What do you want to be when you GROW UP?

Do you ever think about what you'll be when you're older? Try our quiz to find out!

1 After school, you find a very sick dog in the street. Do you take it to the vet? 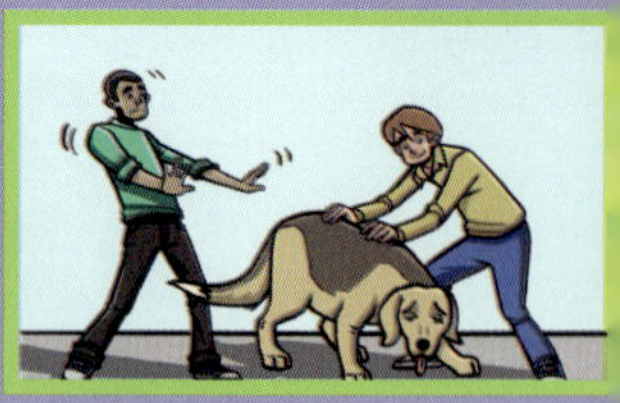
A Are you serious? Look at those teeth. If I go near it, it'll bite me.
B Yes, of course. Where's the nearest animal hospital?
C Yes, and then when it's better, I may write a short story about it.

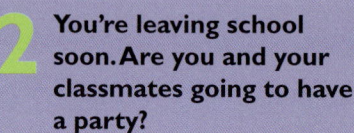

2 You're leaving school soon. Are you and your classmates going to have a party? 
A No. I don't really like parties. I'm going to study for university.
B Yes, I'm going to make sure everybody has a good time.
C Yes, we are. I'm going to make a poster.

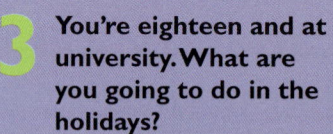

3 You're eighteen and at university. What are you going to do in the holidays? 
A I'm going to stay at home and study for the next year of the course!
B A playgroup near my home needs volunteers. I'm going to look after children.
C What? I'm not going to think about university until I'm 20. I'm going to take a year out and travel around the world.

4 You finish university. What next? 
A I'm sure I'll get a job in a big company. Then I'll get married and have children.
B Perhaps I'll take a year out and work for a charity.
C I think I'll write an article about student life.

Language focus 1 *be going to*

1 Complete the examples from the text on page 64.

	I	we / you / they	he / she / it
+	I ¹…. stay at home.	You **are going to** study in London.	She **is going to** get a job.
−	I ²…. think about university until …	They **aren't going to** take a year out.	He **isn't going to** go to university.
?	**Am** I **going to** get married?	**Are** ³…. have a party?	**Is** he **going to** take a year out?

→ **Grammar reference** • page 105

2 Write sentences about you with the correct form of *be going to*.
1. I / get married / before I go to university
   I'm not going to get married before I go to university.
2. We / watch a film in class / tomorrow
3. My parents / go to the cinema / at the weekend
4. My friends and I / travel around the world / before we go to university
5. I / buy a sports car / when I grow up
6. My aunt / come to stay with us / next week

will vs. *be going to*

3 Complete the examples from the text on page 64. Then choose the correct headings (3–4).

3	Intentions / Predictions

Perhaps I ¹…. take a year out.

4	Intentions / Predictions

I ²…. stay at home and study.

→ **Grammar reference** • page 105

👁 Get it right!

When we make a decision in the moment or we offer to help someone, we use *will*:
A: I can't do my homework.
B: Don't worry, I**'ll** help you. ✓
I'm going to help you. ✗

FACT! Many young people from around the world take a year out between school and university. They call it a 'gap year'. It's a time to have new experiences, travel and learn about life in different countries.

4 🔊 **2.12** Complete the conversation with the correct form of *be going to* or *will* and the verb in brackets. Then listen and check.

Dan: My brother ¹…. (go) to university next year.
Jane: I ²…. (not/go) to university until I'm much older.
Dan: What ³…. you …. (do) instead?
Jane: I ⁴…. (take) a year out. I want to travel around the world.
Dan: That's a good idea! I'm sure you ⁵…. (have) a great time.
Jane: I ⁶…. (go) to the cinema later. Do you want to come?
Dan: I can't. I ⁷…. (study) all afternoon. I've got an exam on Monday.
Jane: OK. Good luck! I'm sure you ⁸…. (pass).
Dan: Thanks.

→ **Say it right!** • page 97

Your turn

5 Complete the sentences so they are true for you with the correct form of *will* or *be going to*.
1. After this class, my classmates and I *are going to have lunch* .
2. If I don't do my homework tonight, my teacher …. .
3. At the weekend, I …. .
4. Next summer, my family …. .
5. When I go to university, I think I …. .
6. I'm sure I …. before I get married or have children.

6 Work with a partner. Ask and answer questions about your sentences in Exercise 5.
A: What are you and your friends going to do after this class?
B: We're going to have lunch. What about you?

Learn about studying at home.
- How old is Maggy?
- Why do Maggy's parents teach their children at home?
- What does Maggy want to be when she grows up?

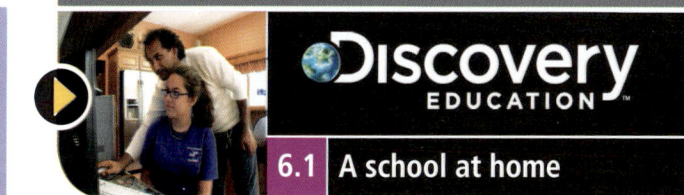

Discovery EDUCATION
6.1 A school at home

Listening A conversation

1 Olivia is showing Lisa a photo of her brother Matt. What do you think he's doing?

2 🔊 2.16 Listen to Lisa and Olivia talking about the photo. Check your ideas to Exercise 1.

3 🔊 2.16 Listen again. Complete the sentences.
   1 Olivia's brother Matt is in ...*Kenya*... .
   2 He's collecting and recycling ..... .
   3 He's going to South Africa to visit ..... .
   4 In South Africa, he wants to get a job in a ..... .
   5 In her year out, Olivia wants to go to ..... .
   6 Lisa would like to ..... in the future.

Vocabulary Containers and materials

4 🔊 2.17 Match the pictures with the words in the box. Then listen, check and repeat.

> plastic bag   cartons   cardboard box   glass jars
> cans   paper bag   crisp packets   plastic bottles

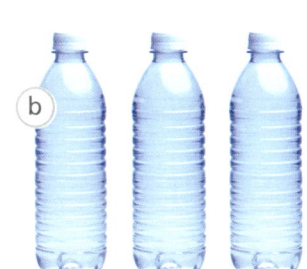

Your turn

5 Work with a partner. How can we reuse the containers in Exercise 4? Write sentences.
We can use glass jars to grow plants. We can fill plastic bottles with sand and use them for bowling.

6 Work in small groups. Compare your sentences from Exercise 5. Who can think of the most unusual ways to reuse the containers?

> We can use glass jars to grow plants.

> That's a good idea. We can also fill plastic bottles with sand and use them for bowling.

➡ Vocabulary bank • page 113

Language focus 2 Present continuous for future

1 Complete the examples from the listening on page 66. Then answer the question below.
  1 He .... to South Africa.
  2 We've got family there, he .... with our cousins.

  1 Do these sentences talk about the present or the future?

➡ **Grammar reference** • page 105

2 🔊 **2.18** Complete the conversations with the present continuous. Then listen and check.
  1 A: Who *are you talking* (you / talk) to?
     B: Francesca, ... (she / ask) about the party tomorrow.
  2 A: .... (you / go) to the cinema this evening?
     B: No, I'm not. .... (I / stay) at home to watch the football.
  3 A: .... (Jonathan / work) at the moment?
     B: No, ... (he / not work). .... (he / study) for his final exams.
  4 A: When .... (Mel / start) her new job?
     B: Next week.
  5 A: When .... (they / leave) for Thailand?
     B: .... (they / fly) to Bangkok next week.
  6 A: Why .... (you / save) money?
     B: .... (I / go) on a trip to Brazil.

3 Which sentences in Exercise 2 talk about the present? Which talk about the future?

4 Look at the photo. What do you think the young woman's job is?

5 Read the text and check your ideas to Exercise 4.

> Charlotte Beck [1] .... (work) in London at the moment. She [2] .... (ask) a politician some questions for the news on TV tonight. Tomorrow she [3] .... (fly) to Washington DC in the USA. The President [4] .... (speak) at an important press conference and she wants to ask him some questions. Lots of journalists and reporters [5] .... (go). Afterwards, she [6] .... (meet) some friends in Washington. Together they [7] .... (fly) to Florida for a short holiday. But she [8] .... (not stay) in Florida for very long. On Sunday she [9] .... (come) back to London because it's her mum's birthday.

6 Complete the text in Exercise 5 with the present continuous form of the verbs in brackets.

Your turn

7 Complete the diary for next week with five activities. Use the words in the box or your own ideas.

> go skiing   ~~play tennis~~   see a concert
> fly to Paris   do an exam   clean the house
> visit a museum

	MORNING	AFTERNOON
MONDAY	play tennis	
TUESDAY		
WEDNESDAY		
THURSDAY		
FRIDAY		

8 Work with a partner. Ask and answer questions about your plans for next week. Can you find a time to meet?

  What are you doing on Monday morning?

  I'm playing tennis. Do you want to come?

Discover Culture

1. Work with a partner. Look at the pictures. Which of the places in the pictures would you most like to visit? Why?

2. Work with a partner. Write down three things you think you will see in Italy, South Africa and Madagascar in the video.

Find out about places around the world.

6.2 Time for an adventure!

3. ▶ 6.2 Watch the video without sound and check your answers to Exercise 2.

4. Which activities can you do in Italy, South Africa and Madagascar? Complete the table with the words in the box.

> help hurt or sick animals   learn to cook
> help look for dinosaur bones
> visit a village and meet people my age
> help to repair old buildings   go hiking

Italy	South Africa	Madagascar
…	help hurt or sick animals, …	…

5. ▶ 6.2 Watch the video again with sound and check your answers to Exercise 4.

6. Test your memory. Choose the best summary of the video.
   1. The girl knows exactly where she is going to go on her gap year.
   2. She has no idea what she is going to do.
   3. She has a few options but she is not sure what will happen.

Your turn

7. What activities can young people on a gap year do in your country? Write down three ideas.
   They can visit the museum, they can learn some words in our language, …

8. Work in small groups. Compare your ideas from Exercise 7. Then choose the best three.

> They can visit the museum.

> That's true. They can also learn some words in our language.

68

Reading An article

1 Look at the map and photos. Laura's taking a year out to spend three months in Goa. Where is Goa?

2 🔊 **2.19** Read the magazine article. Check your ideas to Exercise 1.

3 Read the article again and answer the questions.
   1 Where is Laura working in Goa?
   2 When did Laura arrive in India?
   3 What did Laura learn when she first got there?
   4 What does Laura do in the morning?
   5 What do the children have for lunch?
   6 What are Laura's plans for the afternoon?

Explore verbs with prepositions

4 Look at the article again. Which prepositions do we use after *wait* and *learn*?

5 Choose the correct prepositions to complete the sentences.
   1 I'd like to take a year out and learn **about** / **on** life in a different country.
   2 I'll wait **of** / **for** you, if you like.
   3 You should spend money **in** / **on** a good bag for your year out.
   4 When I went to India, my parents paid **in** / **for** my ticket.
   5 I was listening **at** / **to** the radio when he arrived.
   6 Last night I dreamt **with** / **about** travelling around the world.

➡ **Vocabulary bank** • page 113

Your turn

6 Work with a partner. You're going to take a year out to work on a project in India. Write a list of the things you'll need to do. Use the words in the box and your own ideas.

> get a passport and visa
> visit the doctor   buy a plane ticket
> find out about the country   go shopping

We'll need to get a passport and a visa first. Then we'll visit the doctor.

7 Work in small groups. Compare your lists from Exercise 6.

> First we're going to get a passport and visa. What about you?

> Yes, but before that we're going to buy some cool clothes.

TWELVE WEEKS
IN THE LIFE OF A VOLUNTEER IN GOA

This week, eighteen year old Laura Byrne tells us about her year out.

Four per cent of the children in India are orphans which means they don't have any parents. And for the next twelve weeks, I'm helping in an orphanage, a home for orphans, in Goa, India.

When I arrived two weeks ago, the project manager was waiting for me at the airport. For the first week, we had Hindi classes. We also learned about Indian culture and our project.

I'm working with the younger children. A lot of them had difficult lives before they came here so we have to make sure that they feel safe and happy with us. In the morning, I help with English classes, reading and Maths. We also play games and sing songs. Then I help them with their lunch which is usually chicken or vegetable curry with rice and chapatti, a flatbread from India.

It's very hot here so people wear loose clothes. Women often wear colourful saris made of silk or cotton and men wear dhotis, a kind of long white skirt. This afternoon the older girls are going to show me how to put on a sari.

> **FACT!** *Curry is a dish of meat, fish or vegetables cooked in a spicy sauce. Curry comes from the Tamil word 'Kari' so this dish probably comes from India. However, curry is also one of the national dishes in the UK. There are more curry restaurants in London than in Mumbai.*

Speaking Agreeing and disagreeing

Real talk: What are you going to do when you leave school?

1 ▶ 6.3 Watch the teenagers in the video. Match them with what they're going to do when they leave school.
   a) buy something
   b) be a scientist *Speaker 1*
   c) study a language
   d) learn to drive
   e) work for a charity
   f) play a sport
   g) work
   h) move to another country
   i) be the leader of a country
   j) visit someone

2 What are *you* going to do when *you* leave school? Ask and answer with your partner.

3 🔊 2.20 Listen to the conversation. Why does the reporter want to talk to Katie?

4 🔊 2.20 Complete the conversation with the useful language. Then listen and check your answers.

Useful language

Do you think … ?   Absolutely!   I disagree.
Do you agree?   Maybe, but I (also) think
What's your opinion?   I suppose you're right.

Reporter:	Excuse me! We're looking for young people to tell us their ideas about some different topics.
Katie:	OK. I'll help you. What are the topics?
Reporter:	Well, here's the first one. **All young people should take a year out.** ¹…. ?
Katie:	²…. ! You can learn a lot about life in other countries and also about yourself.
Reporter:	Now, ³…. **everybody should learn to drive**?
Katie	⁴…. we should use bikes, buses and trains more.
Reporter:	But what about **people who live in the countryside**? There aren't any buses there.
Katie:	⁵…. . What's the next one?
Reporter:	**University students should get a job in the holidays.** ⁶…. ?
Katie:	⁷…. ! Students should travel and enjoy themselves. Any more questions?
Reporter:	No, that's it. Thank you very much for your time.

5 Work with a partner. Practise the conversation in Exercise 4.

6 Look at the ideas below and use the useful language to write your opinions.

1 Children shouldn't start school until they're six.

2 Young people should leave home when they're eighteen.

3 It's better to study at a university in another town than one in your town.

4 You should always look for a job where you'll earn a lot of money.

7 Choose three of the ideas from Exercise 6. Change the words in **bold** in the conversation in Exercise 4. Practise the conversation with your partner.

   1 *I'm not sure I agree. I think younger children enjoy playing with their friends.*

Writing A thank you email

1 Read Tom's email. Where is he going on his school trip?

New mail +1

Dear Granny,

Thank you ever so much for the money you gave me for my birthday. I think I'm going to save it for the school trip. The teachers are planning to take us to Paris. We're going to see the Eiffel Tower, some of the museums and maybe we'll spend a day in Disneyland. As you know, I really enjoy visiting new cities so I'm very excited.

Anyway, I have to go. I must finish doing my homework before dinner.

Many thanks again for sending the money and I promise to send you some photos from the trip!

Best wishes,

Tom

---

2 Read Tom's email again and answer the questions.
1. Who is Tom writing to? Why?
2. What present did she give him?
3. What is he going to do with this present?
4. What does he promise to do?

3 Find examples of verb + infinitive and verb + -ing in Tom's email and add the examples to the useful language.

Useful language

Verb patterns
When we use two verbs together, we use:
- an *infinitive with to* after some verbs:
  *I **need to buy** some new shoes*, ¹...., ²....,
- *-ing* after other verbs:
  *I **don't mind travelling** by bus*, ³...., ⁴....,

4 Complete the sentences with the verbs in brackets. Use the infinitive with *to* or *-ing*.
1. You need *to take* an umbrella. It's raining. (take)
2. I don't mind .... early at the weekend. (get up)
3. My brother's planning .... to drive next summer. (learn)
4. I promise .... home before 11 o'clock. (be)
5. I really enjoy ..... I'd like to work in a restaurant. (cook)
6. When I finish .... my room, I'll go out with my friends. (tidy)

Get Writing

PLAN

5 You received some money for your birthday from someone in your family. Make notes about what you want to say in a thank you email. Use the questions in Exercise 2.

WRITE

6 Write your thank you email. Use your notes from Exercise 5, and the language below.

Thank you ever so much for …
I think I'm going to …
As you know, I really enjoy …
Anyway, I have to go. I must …
Many thanks again for …
Best wishes,

CHECK

7 Can you say YES to these questions?
- Have you got verb patterns?
- Have you got the information from Exercise 5?
- Have you got the language from Exercise 6?

5-6 Review

Vocabulary

1 Match the word halves.

microchip

| memory | key | smart | ~~micro~~ | lap | touch |

| screen | top | board | stick | phone | ~~chip~~ |

2 Complete the text with verbs in the box.

| click | log | scroll | shut | turn | sign | turn |

How to check your email
First, ¹.... onto the computer. Then ².... on this icon to open your email account. You need to ³.... into your account and then ⁴.... down the page to see all your messages. You can listen to music while you do this, just ⁵.... up the volume if it's too quiet or ⁶.... down the volume if it's too loud. And when you've finished, just click here to ⁷.... down the computer. Enjoy!

3 Complete the sentences with the words and phrases in the box.

| was born   get a job   learn to drive |
| start school   take a year out   leave home |

1 In my country, children .... when they're five.
2 First, you must ...., and then you can buy a car.
3 My brother would like to live in a flat with his friends so he's going to .... next year.
4 Luke wants to .... and travel around the world before he goes to university.
5 Amy wants to .... in a computer design company.
6 I .... in Scotland but we moved to France when I was three.

4 Match the containers and materials.

| glass (x2)   paper   plastic (x2)   cardboard |

| bottle (x2)   bag (x2)   jar   box |

Explore vocabulary

5 Complete the sentences with the correct adjective form (*-ful* or *-less*) of the nouns in the box.

| beauty   wonder   hope   care   pain   use |

1 I think my team will win the competition. I'm .... .
2 I fell over when I was playing football. Now my leg is very .... .
3 Someone who makes a lot of mistakes is often very .... .
4 My laptop is slow and .... . I can't even sign into my email account.
5 My best friend is tall and .... . She's also very kind and friendly.
6 Last summer, we went to California. I had a .... time there.

6 Choose the correct answers.

1 I'd like to live in Paris when I grow **up** / **off**.
2 Every morning, I get **on** / **up** at 7 am and I put **on** / **out** my school uniform.
3 To get to my school, I get **on** / **up** the bus outside my house and then I get **off** / **out** the bus opposite the park.
4 If I can't find my keys, I look **for** / **at** them under my bed.
5 When you find **out** / **in** the answer to this question, can you write it **up** / **down** here, please?
6 If you buy clothes on the Internet, you can't try them **on** / **out**.

7 Complete the sentences with the correct preposition.

1 If you haven't got enough money, I can pay .... your ticket.
2 My sister always spends her money .... sweets and snacks.
3 Last night, I dreamt .... a large dog. It was chasing me.
4 Please listen .... these instructions carefully.
5 In History, we're learning .... famous explorers.
6 Don't worry if you're late. We can wait .... you.

Language focus

1 Complete the predictions with will/won't, may or might and one of the verbs in the box.

be eat have travel work

1 I'm sure everyone .... at home, not in offices.
2 I'm not certain but people .... robots in their homes.
3 I'm certain we .... to the moon for our holidays.
4 People .... food, they will drink special liquids.
5 There .... cities on Mars but I'm not sure.

2 Match the sentence halves.

1 If you get a smaller computer, …
2 If I don't study this evening, …
3 If you don't do it faster, …
4 My parents will be angry …

a I won't pass my exam.
b if I lose my mobile phone.
c it will be easier to carry.
d you'll miss the next lesson.

3 Complete the sentences with the correct form of *be going to* and the verbs in brackets.

1 A: ¹.... Sharon .... Australia in the summer? (visit)
   B: No, she ².... She ³.... Japan. (visit)
2 A: When ⁴.... Dave and Ann .... married? (get)
   B: In September. They ⁵.... a big wedding. (not have)

4 Choose the correct answers.

Mark: What ¹**will you / are you going to** do this summer?
Jenny: My cousin ²**will / is going to** visit us and we ³**will / are going to** go to the mountains.
Mark: That sounds nice. I think it ⁴**will / is going to** be fun.
Jenny: Yes. I'm sure we ⁵**will / are going to** have a good time.

5 Complete the sentences with the present continuous form of the verbs in the box. Are they talking about the present or the future?

do go go watch

A: We ¹.... out this evening.
B: Really? Where ² .... you .... ?

A: ³.... Lauren .... her homework at the moment?
B: No, she isn't. She ⁴.... TV.

Language builder

6 Choose the correct answers.

Hi Emma,
Can you please help me with my homework? I need to post my blog entries on to the class website. I signed into the website yesterday but I ¹.... see where to post my blog. We ².... three blogs on the class website before Friday. Miss Ross explained how to do it in class and it sounded like ³.... thing to do. I ⁴.... very carefully and now I've got no idea! If I ⁵.... my blog entries, I ⁶.... a mark! What ⁷.... I do? I think it's ⁸.... to give homework to do in our books than online. Do you think in future we ⁹.... our homework on the Internet and we ¹⁰.... paper anymore? Anyway, please help me!
Simon

1 a couldn't   b don't   c shouldn't
2 a 're posting   b will post   c must post
3 a easiest   b the easiest   c the easier
4 a couldn't listen   b wasn't listening c weren't listening
5 a won't post   b don't post   c 'm not posting
6 a didn't get   b won't get   c 'm not getting
7 a should   b did   c will
8 a good   b better   c best
9 a are doing   b will do   c were doing
10 a couldn't use   b are not using   c won't use

Speaking

7 Match the sentences.

1 How does your microphone work?
2 How do I post a message on this forum?
3 I think everyone should learn to drive.
4 My mum says I should work in my free time. Do you agree?
5 Do I need to press that button?

a Maybe, but I also think you should have time to enjoy yourself.
b First, you need to turn it on here.
c Yes, that's it!
d You have to scroll down the page and click on that icon.
e I'm not sure I agree. We should use buses and trains more.

7 Look out!

Discovery EDUCATION

In this unit ...

Danger in our food **p77**

A deadly job **p80**

Accidents **p82**

CLIL Medical myths **p121**

Vocabulary
- Accidents and injuries
- The body
- Expressions with *get*
- Compound nouns

Language focus
- Present perfect
- Present perfect vs. past simple

Unit aims
I can ...
- talk about accidents and injuries.
- talk about the things I have and haven't done in my life.
- understand information about accidents and danger.
- ask and answer questions about the things I have done and say how it happened.
- react to both good and bad news.
- write an email to refuse an invitation.

BE CURIOUS
What can you see in the photo?
Start thinking
- What other dangerous animals can you think of?
- Have you or anyone you know been in a dangerous situation?
- What dangers can you think of in your house?

Vocabulary Accidents and injuries

1 🔊 **2.21** Match the pictures with the words in the box. Then listen, check and repeat.

> hurt your back   bang your head   cut your finger
> slip on ice   break your leg   trip over the dog   crash your car
> fall off your bike   burn your hand   trap your finger

2 Complete the sentences with the correct form of the words in Exercise 1.

1. She _crashed_ her _car_ into a tree. It was a new Lamborghini!
2. I …. my …. with a knife this morning and now it really hurts!
3. Don't touch the plates. They're really hot. You might …. your ….
4. While Dad was moving the wardrobe, he …. his …. . He can't stand up.
5. Tom was jumping over a wall when he fell badly. He …. his …. and he couldn't walk for 6 weeks.
6. Ouch! I always …. my …. on that cupboard on the kitchen wall.

Your turn

3 Write sentences about the last time the accidents and injuries in Exercise 1 happened to you or someone you know.

My mum burnt her hand last week. She was cooking when she touched something hot.

4 Compare your answers with your partner. Can you think of a person for each accident or injury?

➔ **Vocabulary bank** • page 114

AN ACCIDENT WAITING TO HAPPEN

Mick Wilary is a very unlucky man. Over the last 30 years he has had more accidents than anyone else in Britain. He has broken fifteen different bones, and has had more than 30 injuries.

Mick works on a farm and often works with dangerous machines and animals, so some of his accidents have been very serious. In 2010 a machine trapped him and he broke both his legs. He had three operations and spent six months in hospital.

When he was a boy, he fell off a horse. He also got hurt badly when he got home one day, tripped over a cat, fell down the stairs and banged his head.

While working on the farm, he broke his fingers with a hammer and crashed a tractor. But he hasn't only had accidents with machines and animals. 'I'll never forget when Mick stepped on a potato, slipped and broke both his ankles.' his wife Evelyn says.

But Mick has never complained or got angry about his injuries. 'It's important to keep going and get better when these things happen.' he says with a smile. And his wife agrees. 'It's a bit of a joke.'

FACT! In the UK, 33% of all serious injuries happen when someone slips on or trips over something. The government believes it costs hospitals over £100 million to help these people.

Reading A magazine article

1 Work with a partner. Look at the photo of Mick Wilary. How do you think the things below are connected to Mick?

2 🔊 2.22 Read the article and check your ideas to Exercise 1.

3 Mark the sentences true (*T*) or false (*F*).
1 Mick has broken 30 bones this year.
2 In 2010, he broke his legs in an accident in a machine.
3 When he was a boy, he had two accidents with animals.
4 Mick broke his ankles when he slipped on a vegetable.
5 Mick gets angry when something bad happens.

Explore expressions with *get*

4 Look at the article again. Find three examples of *get* + adjective. What does *get* mean in each expression?

5 Complete the sentences with *get* and the words in the box.

> ~~home~~   injured   married   better   sick   worried

1 I always have a sandwich when I *get home* from school.
2 When I'm older, I'm going to …. and have lots of children.
3 Don't climb that tree. You won't be able to play football next week if you …. .
4 When I travel in cars, I usually …. .
5 My parents will …. if I'm home late.
6 My dad has hurt his back. I hope he'll …. soon.

➡ **Vocabulary bank** • page 114

Your turn

6 Write three true or false sentences about you with *get* and the words in the box.

> worried   tired   sick   hurt   old
> home   injured   married   better

I get worried when my dog runs away.

7 Work with a partner. Listen to his/her sentences. Can you guess which are false?

Language focus 1 Present perfect: affirmative and negative

1 Complete the examples from the text on page 76.

I / we / you / they	he / she / it
+ I've had more than 30 serious injuries.	He ¹.... broken fifteen different bones.
− I haven't stopped working on the farm.	He ².... only had accidents with machines.

➡ Grammar reference • page 106

2 Choose the correct words.
1. I have eaten / has eaten fried insects.
2. My grandmother have seen / has seen all the James Bond films.
3. My friends and I haven't swum / hasn't swum in the sea this year.
4. I haven't broken / hasn't broken an arm or a leg.
5. My cousins have flown / has flown in a hot air balloon.
6. My little brother haven't hurt / hasn't hurt himself today!

👁 Get it right!

The past participles of *go* are **been** and **gone**.
We use **been** when someone goes and returns:
I'm sorry I'm late. I've been to the dentist.
We use **gone** when someone hasn't returned:
Jack isn't here today. He's gone to the hospital to visit his grandmother.

3 🔊 2.23 Complete the conversations with the present perfect form of the verbs in brackets and where necessary, *never*. Then listen and check.

1. A: I ¹ *'ve never sung* (✗ sing) in a concert. What about you?
   B: I ².... (✓ sing) in a concert and I ³.... (✓ play) the piano too.
2. A: My cousin ⁴.... (✓ have) a lot of accidents, but she ⁵.... (✗ break) her arm or leg.
   B: That's lucky! My brother ⁶.... (✓ break) his leg twice.
3. A: I ⁷.... (✗ meet) anybody famous, have you?
   B: Well, I ⁸.... (✓ play) football with Cristiano Ronaldo.
   A: Really? Where?
   B: On a computer game!
4. A: I ⁹.... (✗ go) to New York, have you?
   B: Yes, I ¹⁰.... (✓ go) there twice!

4 Write sentences with the correct form of the present perfect and the words below.
1. I / not go / to hospital
2. My parents / visit / 20 countries
3. London / have / the Olympic Games three times
4. Patrick / not read / many books
5. Anna / live / in the USA
6. You / not meet / my cousin Sam

Your turn

5 Write sentences about what you have and haven't done in your life. Use the words in the box or your own ideas.

eat a snake   swim in a cold lake   be on TV
go to another country   write a blog
speak English outside class   go scuba diving

I have never eaten a snake.

6 Work with a partner. Compare your sentences from Exercise 5. Have you done the same things?

> I have never eaten a snake. What about you?

> No, I have never eaten a snake but I've swum in a cold lake. How about you?

7 Write five sentences about your partner.
Anna has never eaten a snake but she has ...

Learn about how 71 people in the USA got E. coli O157.
- What is E. coli O157?
- How do people get it?
- What did the 71 people with E. coli O157 all eat?

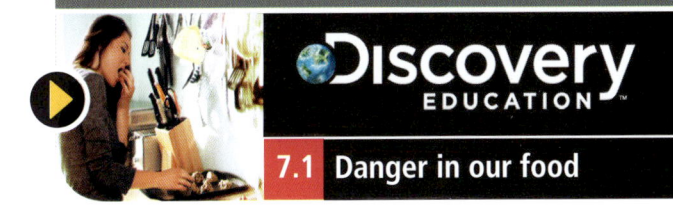

Discovery EDUCATION
7.1 Danger in our food

UNIT 7

Listening A radio interview

1 Work with a partner. Look at the photos. What do you think the most common accidents are to happen in these rooms?

2 🔊 2.24 Listen to the radio interview and check your ideas to Exercise 1.

3 🔊 2.24 Listen again. Mark the sentences true (*T*) or false (*F*). Correct the false sentences.
   1 Over 2 million people have injured themselves at home this year.
   2 Angela thinks the living room is the most dangerous room in the house.
   3 The presenter has never had an accident in the kitchen.
   4 The bathroom can be dangerous for older people and young children.
   5 The most common accident at home is cutting your finger.
   6 Angela's husband fell out of the window last week.

Vocabulary The body

4 🔊 2.25 Match the words in the box with the parts of the body in the picture. Then listen, check and repeat.

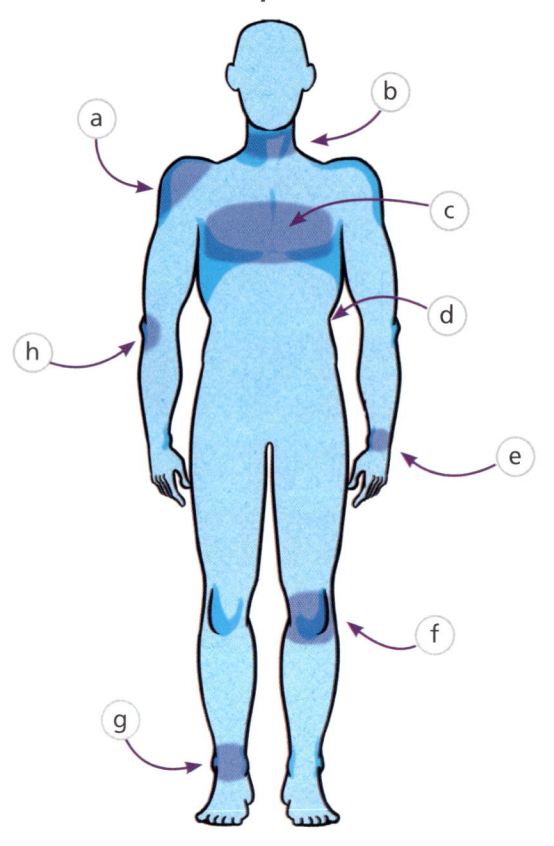

> elbow   ankle   shoulder   neck
> knee   wrist   back   chest

Your turn

5 Write sentences about the parts of your body you have injured. Use the verbs below or your own ideas.

> hurt   break   cut   burn

I've broken my wrist, I've burnt my arm, …

6 Work with a partner. Point to a part of your body. Can your partner guess what happened?

> You've broken your wrist.

> Yes, I have. I fell over when I was skiing.

➡ Vocabulary bank • page 114

Language focus 2 Present perfect: questions

1 Complete the examples from the listening on page 78.

	I / we / you / they	he / she / it
Wh- ?	Where **have** most accidents **happened**?	What **has** he **injured**?
Y/N ?	¹.... you ever .... an accident in the kitchen?	⁴.... he .... any accidents this year?
Short answers	Yes, I ².... . No, I ³.... .	Yes, he ⁵.... . No, he **hasn't**.

➡ Grammar reference • page 106

2 Write questions with the correct form of the present perfect and *ever*.
1 you / lose your keys? *Have you ever lost your keys?*
2 your parents / live in another city?
3 your best friend / go to another country?
4 you / slip on anything?
5 your dad / win a competition?
6 you / watch an important sports match in a stadium?

Your turn

3 Work with a partner. Ask and answer the questions in Exercise 2.

> Have you ever lost your keys?

Past simple vs. present perfect

4 Look at the examples from the listening on page 78 and the rules below. Then complete the table and the rules with past simple or present perfect.

| 1 .... | I'**ve cut** my fingers a few times, and I'**ve burnt** my hand with boiling water. |
| 2 .... | He **fell off** a chair last week. |

We use the ¹.... to say when something happened. We use words like *last week, yesterday, two weeks ago*.
We use the ².... if we don't know when something happened or it's not important when something happened. We use words like *ever, never, in the last ten years, in my life*, etc.

➡ Grammar reference • page 106
➡ Say it right! • page 97

5 Choose the correct words.
1 It's **stopped** / **stopped** raining. Let's ride our bikes.
2 I **haven't tried** / **didn't try** snowboarding. I'd love to do that.
3 My mum**'s read** / **read** six books when we were on holiday.
4 When **have you started** / **did you start** to learn English?
5 **Have you ever had** / **Did you ever have** an accident?
6 My brother**'s finished** / **finished** primary school a few years ago.

6 🔊 **2.27** Complete the text with the present perfect or past simple form of the verbs in brackets. Then listen and check.

My dad and I ¹.... (climb) a lot of mountains and of course it can be dangerous. I ².... (start) when I was 14 but I ³.... (never have) a serious accident. My dad and I ⁴.... (travel) all over the world and we ⁵.... (see) some wonderful things. Last year, we ⁶.... (go) to Argentina. So, where next? We'd love to go to the Himalayas because we ⁷.... (never climb) Everest.

Your turn

7 Work with a partner. Write questions with the present perfect and *ever*. Use these words or your own ideas.

> have a pet   try Mexican food   climb a mountain
> sing Karaoke   skate down a hill

Have you ever had a pet?

8 Change partners. Ask and answer your questions from Exercise 7.

> Have you ever had a pet?

> Yes, I have. My family had a dog a few years ago.

Discover Culture

1 **Work with a partner. Look at the pictures and guess the answers to the questions.**
   1 Which do you think is the most dangerous snake in the world?
   2 How quickly do you think you can you die from a bite from this snake?
   3 Which of the snakes do you think lives in Australia?

Brown

Taipan

Cobra

Find out about snake catchers in Australia.

7.2 A deadly job

2 **7.2 Watch the video and check your answers. Which other animals appear in the video? Which of them are dangerous?**

3 **Test your memory. Match the animals with the actions.**
   1 kangaroos   a yawning
   2 koala   b lying in a box
   3 crocodile   c jumping out of the river
   4 taipan snake   d moving on a rock
   5 brown snake   e eating

4 **7.2 Watch the video again. Check your answers to Exercise 3 and choose the best option to complete the sentences.**
   1 Snakes are a big problem in **Melbourne / Adelaide**.
   2 The snakes go into people's homes **for food / to sleep**.
   3 The *Snake-Away* company take snakes away in a **box / bag**.
   4 They catch the snake by its **tail / head**.
   5 They don't kill the snakes because it's **against the law / unkind**.

Your turn

5 **Look at the dangerous jobs. Write a sentence saying if you would or wouldn't like to do each one and why/why not.**

   snake catcher   firefighter   pilot   racing car driver
   zookeeper   deep sea diver   police officer

   I wouldn't like to be a snake catcher because I'm frightened of snakes.

6 **Work in small groups. Compare your sentences. Do you agree with each other?**

   I wouldn't like to be a snake catcher because I'm frightened of snakes.

   I disagree. That's a really exciting job and you can help people.

Reading An article

1 Look at the photo and answer the questions.
1. Where do tigers live?
2. Which country do you think the photograph shows?
3. Why do you think tigers are dangerous?

2 🔊 2.28 Read the article. Check your ideas to Exercise 1.

3 Read the article again. Answer the questions.
1. What do people do in the forests in the Sundarbans every day?
2. Why is it dangerous for the people to go into the forests?
3. What did the tigers do in the Sundarbans last year?
4. How is the tiger charity helping the people?
5. What should you do if you see a tiger?
6. How is the tiger a part of the culture in the region?

Explore compound nouns

4 Look at the words in **bold** in the article. What do they mean?

5 Match the words in the box to the definitions.

> forest floor   firewood   wildlife
> charity worker   fishing boat

1. Wood that you use to make a fire.
2. A boat that you use when you go fishing.
3. People who work for a charity.
4. The ground in the forest.
5. The animals, birds and plants that live in an area.

➡ **Vocabulary bank** • page 114

Your turn

6 Write your answers to the questions.
1. What dangerous animals, plants or birds are there in your country?
2. Have you or anyone you know ever had a bad experience with an animal? What happened?

7 Work in small groups. Compare your answers from Exercise 6.

LIVING WITH TIGERS

In the Sundarbans region in Bangladesh, thousands of people go into the forests every day to fish, hunt and look for honey and **firewood**. The work is difficult and it can also be very dangerous because the forests are home to lots of **wildlife**, including about 400 tigers.

In the last year, tigers have killed about 50 people in the Sundarbans area. The local people feel scared and they worry that the tigers will come into their villages and attack them. They sometimes go into the forests and kill the tigers.

With the help of a tiger charity, local people are learning how to live and work close to tigers, how to look for tiger marks on the **forest floor** and listen for the sounds from other animals when there is a tiger nearby. **Charity workers** also tell people where the attacks have happened. If they see a tiger, they learn not to run away, but to look at it and make lots of noise.

The tiger is a big part of the culture here. The people sing songs about tigers and tell stories about tiger gods. The charity hopes that the people will learn to understand the tigers better, and will be able to live safely with these beautiful animals.

FACT! There are only about 3,000 wild tigers left in the whole world.

Speaking Reacting to news

Real talk: Have you ever had an accident?

1 ▶ 7.3 Watch the teenagers in the video and complete the table.

	Speaker 1	Speaker 2	Speaker 3	Speaker 4	Speaker 5	Speaker 6
Have you ever had an accident?	Yes	....	....	....	....	....
What did you hurt?	my ankle	....	....	....	....	....

2 Have *you* ever had an accident? Ask and answer with your partner.

3 🔊 2.29 Listen to Holly talking to Theo. Who has the best news?

4 🔊 2.29 Complete the conversation with the useful language. Then listen and check your answers.

5 Work with a partner. Practise the conversation in Exercise 4.

6 Work with a partner. Tell each other some good news and bad news. Use the ideas below or you own. Use the useful language to react to the news.

> What have you been up to?

> I won a writing competition last week.

> Well done! That's fantastic.

Useful language

What have you been up to?   I've (*passed all my exams*).
How's it going?   Oh no!
How (*amazing*)!   What a shame!
That's (*fantastic*)!   I'm sorry to hear that.

Theo: Hi Holly. ¹.... ?
Holly: Fine, thanks. How about you?
Theo: Yeah, not bad. ².... passed all my exams.
Holly: Well done! ³.... !
Theo: Thanks! The exams weren't easy. ⁴.... ?
Holly: Well, my brother's had an accident. He's broken his leg.
Theo: ⁵.... . Is it serious?
Holly: No, not really. He's at home now. His football team's in the final but he can't play.
Theo: ⁶.... ! ⁷.... .
Holly: Yes. But my other news is that **we're going to Thailand for our holidays**.
Theo: Wow! ⁸.... ! I think I'm going to **summer school**.
Holly: Really? Lucky you!

TEAM WINS IMPORTANT MATCH

WIN A WRITING COMPETITION

DO A 10KM RUN FOR CHARITY

HAVE AN ACCIDENT

LOSE SOMETHING VALUABLE

FAIL EXAMS

Writing An email refusing an invitation

1 Look at the photo and read the email. Why is Gemma writing to Ted?

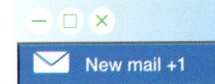

Hi Ted,

I'm really sorry but I'm afraid I can't come on the trip to the amusement park this Saturday because I've had an accident.

I fell off my bicycle and broke my leg when I was cycling to school on Monday. It was really painful. I went to the hospital and they put a plaster on it. Now I can't walk and will have to rest for the next eight weeks! It's terrible.

Could we meet another day? Would you like to come round for lunch on Sunday? It would be great to see you.

I hope you have a fantastic time on Saturday!

Sorry again.

Gemma

---

2 Read Gemma's email again and answer the questions.
1. Where can't Gemma go?
2. Why can't she go?
3. What does she need to do now?
4. What new plan does she suggest?

Useful language

Polite language for refusing

When you refuse an invitation, use polite language …
- to apologise *I'm really sorry but …* , ¹……
- to refuse an invitation *I'm afraid I can't …* , ²……
- to suggest another time *Could we meet another day?*, ³……
- to finish the email *I hope you have a fantastic time,* ⁴……

3 Add the examples below to the useful language.

> Enjoy yourselves!
> Sorry for not telling you before.
> How about another day?
> I would love to go but I can't.

Get Writing

PLAN

4 Read the email from your friend Lisa and make notes about why you can't go. Use the questions in Exercise 2.

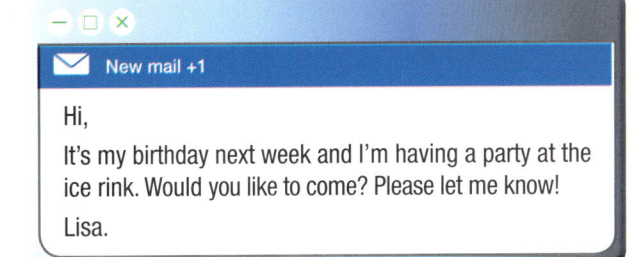

Hi,

It's my birthday next week and I'm having a party at the ice rink. Would you like to come? Please let me know!

Lisa.

WRITE

5 Write your email. Use your notes from Exercise 4, and the language below.

Hi … ,
I'm really sorry but I'm afraid I can't … because …
Could we meet another day?
Shall we …?
I hope you have a fantastic time!
Sorry again.

CHECK

6 Can you say YES to these questions?
- Have you got polite language?
- Have you got the information from Exercise 4?
- Have you got the language from Exercise 5?

8 Having fun!

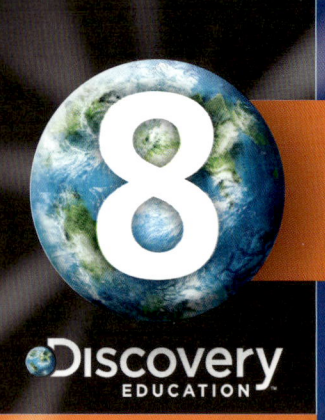

Discovery EDUCATION

In this unit ...

- A New York City food tour p87
- Punkin Chunkin! p90 
- Birthday celebrations p92 
- CLIL An ancient answer p123 

Vocabulary
- Free time activities
- Adjectives of feeling
- Expressions with *have*
- Making nouns from verbs

Language focus
- *one/ones*
- *too* + adjective
- Indefinite pronouns
- *(not)* adjective + *enough*

Unit aims
I can ...
- talk about my free time activities.
- talk about people, things and places without repeating the same words.
- understand information about how people have fun around the world.
- talk about things which are too big, small, cold, etc. or not big, small, cold, etc. enough.
- make suggestions and respond to them.
- write an email invitation to a friend.

BE CURIOUS

What can you see in the photo?

Start thinking
- How are these people feeling?
- How do you and your friends have fun?
- What's the best day out you've ever had?

Vocabulary Free time activities

1 🔊 **2.30** Match the pictures with the words in the box. Then listen, check and repeat.

> play computer games   meet friends
> spend time with your family
> use the Internet   draw pictures
> take photos   read books or magazines
> watch films   have a party
> play an instrument

2 Complete the questions with the correct form of the verbs in Exercise 1.
1. What kind of computer games do you …. ?
2. Did you …. a party on your last birthday?
3. What books or magazines have you …. this week?
4. When do you …. time with your family?
5. Are you going to …. the Internet later?
6. What instruments can you …. ?
7. Where do you usually …. your friends?
8. Do you and your friends often …. photos with your mobiles?

Your turn

3 Write your answers to the questions in Exercise 2.
1. *I like playing football games.*

4 Work in small groups. Ask and answer the questions in Exercise 2. Remember to ask for more information.

> What kind of computer games do you play?

> I like playing football games.

➡ Vocabulary bank • page 115

85

Reading An online forum

1 Look at the photos and read the introduction to the online forum. What's a long weekend? Which plan do you think you would prefer?

2 🔊 2.31 Read the article and check your ideas to Exercise 1.

3 Read the text again and write *M* (Michele), *R* (Rohun) or *S* (Suzi).
1. Who's spending time with their family?
2. Who's going somewhere with their class?
3. Who's doing something in their school?
4. Who's going somewhere outside?
5. Who's going to have fun in the café?
6. Who's inviting you to listen to music?

Explore expressions with *have*

4 Look at the text again. Find three expressions with *have*.

5 Write sentences about you with *have* and one of the words in the box.

> a good time   a shower   a rest
> a problem   a meal   a party

I had a good time at my friend's party last week.

➡ Vocabulary bank • page 115

Your turn

6 What can you do in your town on a long weekend? Write three ideas.
You can meet your friends at the shopping centre and you can have a drink in the café.

7 Compare your ideas with a partner. Then write a short paragraph for the online forum.

PLANS FOR THE
LONG WEEKEND

No school on Monday so this weekend's going to be a long one! Post your plans for the weekend below.

MICHELE GREEN, YEAR 9
Lunch with my grandparents on Saturday but the next day I'm going to meet my friends at the open-air swimming pool. There's something for everyone there and we always have a good time! If you want a swim, the water's warm. If you want to sit in the sun, there's always somewhere to put your towel. And if you get thirsty, you can have something to drink at the café.

ROHUN PATEL, YEAR 10
I play the guitar in a band with three friends. If you haven't got anything better to do, we're playing two concerts this weekend. The first one is on Saturday at 6 pm in the school hall and tickets are free! Come and join us!

SUZI POLOWETSKY, YEAR 9
I'm going to the library on Saturday with my classmates. No! Not to read books! There's an exhibition for students to show their photos and Misha's taken some amazing ones of our school trip. We're having a party afterwards in the café. Why don't you come?

> **FACT!** The world's largest open-air swimming pool is in Chile. It's more than 1 km long. That's the size of 20 Olympic swimming pools.

Language focus 1 one/ones

1 Complete the examples from the text on page 86.

Singular object	No school on Monday so this weekend's going to be a long ¹.... !
Plural object	Misha's taken some amazing ².... of our school trip.

➡ Grammar reference • page 107

2 🔊 **2.32** Complete the conversations with *one* or *ones*. Then listen and check.

Lucy:	Which ¹.... is your skateboard?
Caroline:	That ².... .
Lucy:	Is it the ³.... with red stars?
Caroline:	No, it's got blue ⁴.... .

Tania:	I like those shoes.
Jenny:	Which ⁵.... ? The ⁶.... on the brown box?
Tania:	No, those shoes on the black ⁷.... .
Jenny:	Oh! I prefer the boots next to those ⁸.... .

Indefinite pronouns

3 Complete the examples from the text on page 86.

	People	Things	Places
affirmative	There's something for ¹.... there.	You can have ².... to drink at the café.	There's always ³.... to put your towel.
negative	There is **nobody** from school at the concert.	If you haven't got ⁴.... better to do.	We don't usually go **anywhere** special at the weekend.

➡ Grammar reference • page 107

👁 Get it right!

Use the verb in the negative with *any*:
I haven't had **anything** to eat. ✓
~~I haven't had nothing to eat.~~ ✗

4 Replace the words in **bold** with an indefinite pronoun.
1 I think there's **a person** at the door. *someone*
2 Where's Jack? He's **in a room** in the school.
3 I've looked for my bag **in all the places** in the house. I can't find it **in any place**.
4 There's **no food** in the fridge.
5 Ouch! I've got **a small object** in my shoe!
6 There's **not one place** we can buy milk.

Your turn

5 Write this information on a piece of paper in a different order.
- someone famous you have met.
- somewhere you've never been.
- someone famous you would like to meet.
- something you've done that you really enjoyed.
- somewhere you've been that was amazing.
- something you've never done that you'd like to do.

New York, Usain Bolt, …

6 Read your partner's information from Exercise 5. Can you guess what it means?

> Is New York somewhere you've never been?

> No, it isn't. It's somewhere I've been that was amazing.

Learn about having a meal in New York.
- What can you eat at Katz's Delicatessen?
- Does Sylvia's Restaurant have Chinese food?
- What does everyone enjoy at Serendipity?

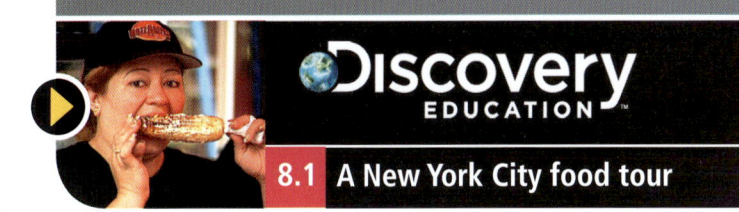

8.1 A New York City food tour

Listening A radio interview

1 Look at the photos of three school trips. Where did the pupils go? What did they do there?

2 🔊 2.33 Listen to the radio interview and check your ideas to Exercise 1.

3 🔊 2.33 Listen again and answer the questions.
1 Did Hannah and her friends take off their coats? Why/Why not?
2 How did Hannah and her classmates feel about the teacher?
3 What did Toby think about the Spanish lesson?
4 Did Toby have fun in the dancing class? Why/Why not?
5 Did Kate have a good time?
6 Why did the little monkey feel sad?

Vocabulary Adjectives of feeling

4 🔊 2.34 Match the pictures a–i with the words in the box. Then listen, check and repeat.

> angry   bored   excited   tired   afraid   upset
> interested   embarrassed   surprised

➡ **Say it right!** • page 97

Your turn

5 Look at the adjectives in Exercise 4. What usually makes you feel this way? Write sentences with the words in the box or your own ideas.

> long weekend   spiders   going on a school trip
> losing an important game or competition
> a very sad book or film   my brother or sister

I feel excited before a long weekend. I feel afraid when …

6 Work with a partner. Ask and answer questions about your sentences in Exercise 5. Do you feel the same way about the same things?

> When do you feel excited?

> I feel excited before a long weekend.

➡ **Vocabulary bank** • page 115

Language focus 2 *too* + adjective

1 Complete the examples from the listening on page 88.

+ It was ¹.... to take off our coats.
  I was ².... to look.

➡ Grammar reference • page 107

2 Complete the sentences with *too + adjective + infinitive*. Use the adjectives in the box.

| hot | cold | late | small | old | young |

1 I'm not going into the sea.
  It's ..*too cold to swim*.. (swim).
2 It's time for bed. It's .... (watch) TV.
3 I'm sorry, but the children are .... (ride) that horse.
4 It's 40 °C today. It's .... (play) tennis.
5 My brother is .... (join) the army. He must wait until he's 18.
6 My granddad is .... (play) football, but he still enjoys watching it.

(*not*) adjective + *enough*

3 Complete the examples from the listening on page 88.

+ The test was easy ¹.... for everyone to pass.
− One of the little monkeys wasn't ².... to get to the table.

➡ Grammar reference • page 107

4 Complete the sentences with (*not*) *enough* and the adjectives in brackets.

1 We can't eat in the garden because it ..*isn't warm enough*.. (warm) to sit outside.
2 You can't go to that disco because you .... (old) to get in.
3 We don't need to go by car because it .... (close) to walk.
4 You mustn't go in the water because it .... (safe) to swim.
5 I only want a snack because I .... (hungry) to eat a big meal.
6 We can drive all of you to the match because our car .... (big) to take seven people.

👁 Get it right!

Use *too* before the adjective.
I'm *too* young to see the film.
Use *enough* after the adjective.
I'm not old *enough* to see the film.

5 Choose the correct words to complete the sentences.

1 Don't go in the sea. It's **not dangerous enough / too dangerous** to swim today.
2 You can't move that box on your own. You're **not strong enough / too strong** to carry it.
3 My sister's staying at home today. She's **not well enough / too well** to go to school.
4 I'm going to bed. I'm **not tired enough / too tired** to watch the film.
5 I wanted to go to the concert but the tickets were **not expensive enough / too expensive** to buy.
6 The wall is **not high enough / too high** to jump over.

6 Order the words to make questions.

1 ice cream / to / too / cold / Is / eat / it / an?
  Is it too cold to eat an ice cream?
2 Have / tired / go out / you / too / to / been / ever?
3 you / Were / hungry / to / big / breakfast / enough / have / a?
4 strong / Are / carry / a / you / to / enough / friend?
5 your / sports team / enough / Is / good / win / to / league / the?
6 house / big / enough / have / Is / your / party / to / a?

Your turn

7 Write your answers to the questions in Exercise 6.

No, it isn't too cold to eat an ice cream. I'd like one, please!

8 Work with a partner. Ask and answer the questions in Exercise 6.

> Is it too cold to eat ice cream?

> No, it isn't too cold to eat an ice cream. I'd like one, please!

Discover Culture

1 **Work with a partner. Look at the pictures and answer the questions.**
   1 Do you ever eat pumpkin? When? What do you eat it with?
   2 What else do you think you could do with a pumpkin?

Find out about a pumpkin competition in Bridgeville, USA.

Discovery EDUCATION

8.2 Punkin Chunkin!

2 **You are going to watch a video about the 'Punkin Chunkin' competition in Bridgeville, USA. What do you think happens in this competition?**

3 ▶ 8.2 **Watch the video and check your answers to Exercise 2.**

4 ▶ 8.2 **Watch the video again and complete the text with the words in the box.**

| champion   festival   fun   pumpkin |
| shoot   mess   chuck |

Some people call it a sport. Some call it a ¹…. But everyone thinks it's ²…. The rules are simple. First, take a ³…. Then build a machine to ⁴… it as far as you can. Jake's father helped to organise the very first Punkin Chunkin ⁵… in 1986. Now the whole family helps ⁶… pumpkins. And Jake is the best. In 2008 he was the world ⁷… and again in 2012. Jake's pumpkins have gone 1,366 metres.

5 **Test your memory. Choose the correct answers.**
   1 Some / All of the machines have the American flag.
   2 None / Some of the machines break.
   3 Some people / Nobody wear(s) strange costumes.
   4 Nobody / Some people celebrate(s) the results.
   5 Some / All of the pumpkins have writing on them.
   6 A lot of / Not many people come to watch the competition.

Your turn

6 **Write down the rules for an unusual competition in your country, or invent one.**
   We've got a cheese throwing competition. First, you need to choose a cheese. Next, you have to …

7 **Work in small groups. Compare your unusual competitions and choose your favourite.**

   I like Marco and Anna's competition best because everyone has a good time.

   I prefer the cheese one because …

Reading An article

1 Work with a partner. Read the quiz and guess the answers.

2 🔊 **2.36** Read the article. Check your answers to the quiz.

Explore making nouns from verbs

3 Look at the article again. Find the noun from the verb *play*. What do we add to the verb to make the noun?

4 Complete the sentences with the correct form of the verbs in the box.

> have a party   ~~play jokes~~   take photos
> use the Internet   play an instrument   watch films

1 *Playing jokes* on 1 April is still normal in English-speaking countries.
2 I think …. on TV is better than going to the cinema.
3 …. on your birthday is a great way to see all your friends and have fun.
4 …. with your mobile is easier than with a camera.
5 …. in a band is hard work if you have to play a concert every weekend.
6 …. on a very small computer screen is difficult.

➡ **Vocabulary bank • page 115**

Your turn

5 Imagine you are a newsreader. Write down two jokes you would like to tell everyone in your country.
I'd like to tell everyone that monkeys can talk.

6 Work with a partner. Compare your jokes and choose the best one.

> I'd like to tell everyone that the moon is made of cheese.

> That's a good one! I'd like to …

APRIL FOOLS' DAY

Be careful! Today is 1 April. Don't listen to your friends when they say school's closed for a week! Don't run to the window if your dad tells you it's snowing. It's April Fools' Day and you don't want to be the fool!

How much do you know about April Fools' Day? QUIZ

1 On April Fools' Day people …
a don't go to school.
b play jokes on each other.
c have a party.

2 Before the 16th Century, New Year's Day was …
a on 1st April.
b on 1st January.
c on two different days.

3 April Fools' Day is …
a only in England.
b only on TV.
c in places where people speak English.

4 Spaghetti
a grows on trees.
b is also a type of tree.
c doesn't grow on trees.

5 Big Ben …
a has now got a digital face.
b is in London.
c is going to change.

People believe that April Fools' Day began in the sixteenth century when New Year's Day moved from 1 April to 1 January. Of course, there wasn't any TV or Internet so people didn't know about this change until several years later. People who continued to celebrate New Year's Day on 1 April were called fools.

Playing jokes on 1 April is still normal in English-speaking countries today. News programmes enjoy the fun too! Here are two of the most famous jokes from the British TV channel, the BBC.

In 1957, they showed a programme about spaghetti growing on trees. A lot of people thought it was true and they phoned the BBC to ask where they could buy the trees.

Then, in 1980, they said that Big Ben, the famous clock in London, had a new digital face. Everyone was very unhappy about the change until the BBC told them it was an April Fools' joke!

FACT! In 2013, a famous internet search engine said that people could now use the Internet to look for different smells. It was one of the most popular April Fools' jokes ever.

Speaking Suggesting and responding

Real talk: How do you celebrate your birthday?

1 ▶ **8.3** Watch the teenagers in the video and write the number of the speaker.
On their birthday, who …
a) likes having a party?
b) goes on trips?
c) spends time with their family at home?
d) had an exam this year?

2 How do *you* celebrate *your* birthday? Ask and answer with your partner.

3 🔊 **2.37** Listen to Paul talking to Molly. Where do they decide to go for his birthday?

4 🔊 **2.37** Complete the conversation with the useful language. Then listen and check your answers.

Useful language

What about (+ *-ing*) …?
Let's (+ infinitive without *to*).
Why don't we (+ infinitive without *to*) …?
That's a great idea!
I'd rather (+ infinitive without *to*) …
How about (+ *-ing*) …?
Where shall we (+ infinitive without *to*) …?
Ok, why not?

Paul:	¹… go for my birthday?
Molly:	²… **going to the beach**? We can **have a picnic**.
Paul:	No, ³… do something more exciting.
Molly:	OK. ⁴… going to **the water park**?
Paul:	No, I've been there a lot. It's boring.
Molly:	Well I don't know! ⁵… look on the Internet for more ideas?
Paul:	⁶… ?
Molly:	Look at this! What about **paintballing**? Have you ever done that?
Paul:	No, never! ⁷… !
Molly:	Well there's a **new place in the park**. It's open **every afternoon**.
Paul:	Fantastic! ⁸… go there.
Molly:	Yes, it'll be fun!

5 Work with a partner. Practise the conversation in Exercise 4.

6 Work with a partner. Change the words in **bold** in the conversation in Exercise 4. Use the pictures below or your own ideas. Then practise the conversation.

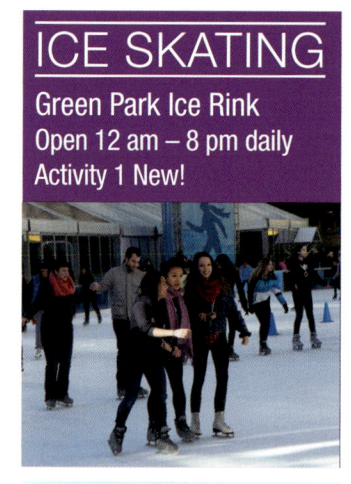

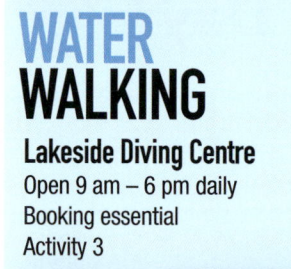

ICE SKATING
Green Park Ice Rink
Open 12 am – 8 pm daily
Activity 1 New!

WATER WALKING
Lakeside Diving Centre
Open 9 am – 6 pm daily
Booking essential
Activity 3

SEGWAY EXCURSION
NEW FOREST FUN
Open 10 am – 5 pm
Weekends only
Activity 2 New!

HORSE RIDING
Blackthorn Riding Stables
Open weekdays: 2–7 pm
Weekends 9 am – 6 pm
Activity 4

UNIT 8

Writing An email invitation to a friend

1 Look at the photo and read Sara's email. What is she planning to do?

Hi Lola,
How are things? Sorry I haven't phoned you. We've had exams all week but we've finished ¹ **them** now. The Maths and History ² **ones** were really hard.
Anyway, my friends and I are having a meal to celebrate the end of the school year and ³ **we**'d like you to come. ⁴ **It**'s on 23 June at Mario's Restaurant. That's the ⁵ **one** behind the cinema. They've got great pizza ⁶ **there**. There'll be dancing afterwards – I know you'll love ⁷ **that**!
We're meeting outside Mario's at 7 pm. I hope you can come. I have to book the restaurant on Thursday. Please let me know what you think before ⁸ **then**.
Sara
PS Everyone would love to see you!

---

2 Read Sara's email again and answer the questions.
1. What are Sara and her friends celebrating?
2. How are they going to celebrate? Where?
3. Are they going to do anything afterwards?
4. What time are they meeting for the celebration?
5. When does Lola need to tell Sara if she can go to the celebration?

Useful language

Referencing words
We often use referencing words so we don't repeat the noun:
- I took **my new bag** to the party, but I left **it** (my new bag) **there** (at the party).
- I can't find **my red pen**. Have you got **one** (a red pen)?
- There's **pizza** for dinner. I know you like **that** (pizza).
- I'm having a party on **Saturday**. I have to buy some food before **then** (Saturday).

3 Find examples of referencing words in **bold** in the email. What does each one mean?
1. *the exams*

4 Look at the useful language and write a referencing word for the words in **bold**.
1. I'm still doing **my homework** but I've nearly finished *it*.
2. I'm going to the concert with **Kate**. ..... 're meeting at the theatre.
3. I'd like to see **an adventure film**. Is there ..... on at the cinema?
4. 'Shall we **play cards** after dinner?' 'Yes, I'd love ..... .'
5. 'Let's meet outside **the cinema** at 8.30.' 'OK. See you ..... .'
6. I've got a football match on **Friday**. I need to buy some new football boots before ..... .

Get Writing

PLAN

5 Make notes about your own celebration. Use the questions in Exercise 2.

WRITE

6 Write your email. Use your notes from Exercise 5 and the language below.

How are things?
Sorry I haven't …
My friends and I are … and we'd like you to come.
It's on … at …
We're meeting …
I hope you can come.
I have to book … on …
Please let me know before then.

CHECK

7 Can you say YES to these questions?
- Have you got referencing words?
- Have you got the information from Exercise 5?
- Have you got the language from Exercise 6?

7–8 Review

Vocabulary

1 Match the sentences halves.
1. There's a lot of ice outside …
2. That box is heavy …
3. The iron is hot …
4. This knife is very sharp …
5. The cupboard is very low …
6. Ride carefully …

a don't fall off your bike.
b don't cut your finger.
c don't hurt your back.
d don't burn your hand.
e don't slip on it.
f don't bang your head.

2 Write the name of each part of the body in the picture.

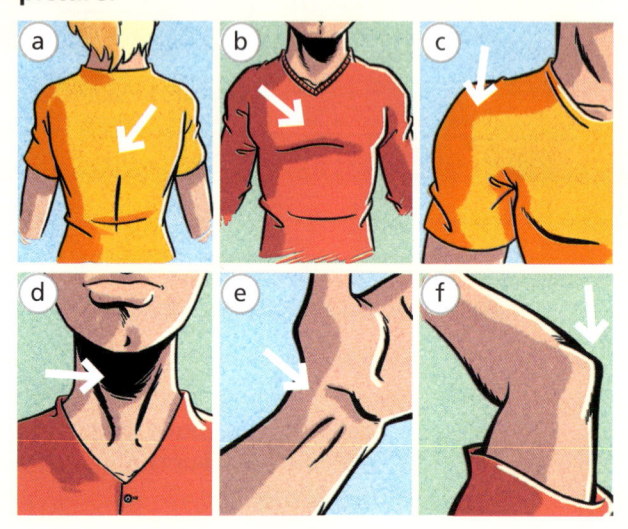

a b c
d e f

3 Match the verbs with the nouns.
1. use
2. spend
3. take
4. read
5. draw
6. meet

a books or magazines
b the Internet
c pictures
d friends
e time with your family
f photos

4 Complete the sentences with the adjectives in the box.

> bored   excited   embarrassed
> afraid   tired   angry

1. Susan's really …. . She went to bed very late last night.
2. Tim is …. of spiders. Especially big ones!
3. Nina is …. . Her younger sister has broken her new mobile phone.
4. Chris is …. with his new computer game. He's played it hundreds of times.
5. Kylie is …. . It's her birthday tomorrow and she's having a party.
6. Alex is …. . He has to sing in the school play and he doesn't like singing.

Explore vocabulary

5 Complete the sentences with *get* or *have* and one of these words.

> a rest   a shower   sick   injured
> a good time   worried

1. Snowboarding is quite dangerous. A lot of people …. .
2. If I don't get home soon, my parents will …. .
3. I'm tired. I'm going to lie down and …. .
4. I meet my friends on Friday afternoon. We always …. .
5. If you don't sleep or eat well, you'll …. .
6. Before breakfast, I always …. and put on my clothes.

6 Read the descriptions of some compound nouns. What is the word for each one?
1. The people who work for a charity.
   c _ _ _ _ _ _ _ w _ _ _ _ _ _
2. The animals, birds, plants that live in an area.
   w _ _ _ _ _ _ _ _
3. Fishermen use this boat to go fishing.
   f _ _ _ _ _ _ b _ _ _
4. This is the ground in a forest.
   f _ _ _ _ _ f _ _ _ _
5. This is the wood that we use to make fires.
   f _ _ _ _ _ _ _

7 Complete the sentences with the noun form (*-ing*) of the verbs in the box.

> play an instrument   have a party
> watch films   use the Internet
> play jokes   take photos

1. …. on TV at home with my friends is great fun.
2. The best way to enjoy your birthday is …. with all your friends.
3. …. in the school band is a good way to make new friends.
4. …. of all the new places is a good way to remember your holiday.
5. …. on your friends can make them laugh or make them very angry.
6. …. on an old, slow computer isn't a good idea.

94

Language focus

1 Complete the sentences with the present perfect simple form of the verbs in brackets.

1 I .... (not fall off) a bike, but I .... (fall off) a horse.
   I haven't fallen off a bike, but I've fallen off a horse.
2 He .... (break) his arm, but he .... (not break) his leg.
3 She .... (be) skiing, but she .... (not be) surfing.
4 We .... (read) a lot of magazines, but we .... (not read) many books.

2 Write questions with the present perfect and the words below.

1 you / ever / play / an instrument in a concert?
2 your parents / visit / a lot of countries?
3 your brother / ever / climb / a mountain?
4 your sister / ever / win / a competition?
5 you / ever / find / money on the floor?

3 Choose the correct answers.

Jim: ¹ **Have you ever burnt / Did you ever burn** your hand?
Sophie: Yes, I ² **have / did**. I ³ **'ve burnt / burnt** it last week.
Jim: How ⁴ **have you done / did you do** it?
Sophie: When I was making breakfast, I ⁵ **'ve put / put** my hand on the cooker.

4 Complete the sentences with *one* or *ones*.

1 A: Which bag do you want?
   B: The blue ...., please.
2 A: Are these your shoes?
   B: No, my shoes are the black .....
3 A: Which biscuits do you want?
   B: Which .... are the best?

5 Choose the correct answers.

1 It's very quiet. I can't hear **something / anything**.
2 We're going **anywhere / somewhere** for a day out.
3 The room is empty. There isn't **someone / anyone** here.
4 Let's find **somewhere / nowhere** to sit down.

6 Complete the sentences with *too* or *not enough* and the adjective in brackets.

1 Let's go to bed. It's .... (late) to watch a film now.
2 Can you help me? I'm .... (strong) to carry this box.
3 Put on some jeans! It's .... (warm) to wear shorts.
4 These shoes are .... (big) for me. I need a smaller size.
5 I can't see the band very well. I'm .... (tall).

UNIT 7–8

Language builder

7 Choose the correct answers.

Jill: What ¹.... tonight?
Jack: I ².... out with some friends to see my cousin's band. She's the singer. I think she sings ³.... than many other famous people.
Jill: Cool! Have you ever ⁴.... in a band?
Jack: No, I haven't but I ⁵.... the piano when I was younger.
Jill: So ⁶.... a CD?
Jack: Yes! They recorded ⁷.... at a concert and posted it on the Internet. ⁸.... you want to come to the concert with us?
Jill: Yes, please! I ⁹.... ask my parents first. If they say I can go, I ¹⁰.... you a message.
Jack: Great! Hope to see you later.

	a	b	c
1	do you do	are you doing	will you do
2	'm going	go	will go
3	beautifully	more beautiful	more beautifully
4	sing	sang	sung
5	play	could play	've played
6	did they make	were they making	have they made
7	one	ones	them
8	Do	Would	Are
9	may	must	mustn't
10	'll send	send	sent

Speaking

8 Complete the conversations with the words in the box.

> That's a great idea   What a shame!
> How's it going?   Where shall we   I'd rather
> That's amazing!   Why don't we

Kate: Hi Ian! ¹....
Ian: Great! We've just won the football league!
Kate: Well done! ²..... My team lost their match.
Ian: ³....!

Matt: ⁴.... go tomorrow?
Fiona: ⁵.... go swimming? The new pool's just opened.
Matt: ⁶.... go ice skating.
Fiona: ⁷.....

Say it right!

Unit 1 /f/

The final sound in *enough* is pronounced /f/.

1 🔊 1.08 **Listen and repeat.**

/f/ enough

2 **Which of the following words also have this sound?**

of laugh elephant through coffee phone off

3 🔊 1.09 **Listen and check.**

4 **Write down ten more words that have the sound /f/.**

5 **How many ways can you spell the sound /f/?**

Unit 2 Irregular verbs

1 🔊 1.16 **Listen and repeat the irregular past simple verbs.**

read thought came had drank left
ate saw sat gave taught said

2 **Put the verbs in the correct column.**

/e/ red	/ɔ:/ four	/æ/ cat	/ei/ train
read, …			

3 🔊 1.17 **Listen and check your answers.**

4 **Work with a partner. Talk about what you did yesterday. Use the irregular verbs above.**

> Yesterday morning, I saw my friends at school. In the evening, I ate dinner with my parents, and then I read my book.

Unit 3 was/were

1 🔊 1.24 **Listen to the questions and answers. How do we say *was* and *were*?**

Detective:	What were you doing between 8 and 8.30 last night?
Schoolboy:	I was looking at my Maths book.
Detective:	Why were you studying Maths?
Schoolboy:	Because I've got an exam tomorrow.
Detective:	Where were you sitting?
Schoolboy:	In my bedroom.
Detective:	Were you talking to anyone at the same time?
Schoolboy:	No, I was doing it alone.

2 🔊 1.24 **Listen and repeat the dialogue.**

3 **Work with a partner. Practise the dialogue.**

Unit 4 schwa

1 🔊 1.31 **Listen to the sentences. How do we pronounce the letters in bold?**
  1 France is small**er** th**a**n Brazil.
  2 I'm bett**er** **a**t Maths th**a**n **a**t History.
  3 This classroom is bigg**er** th**a**n our classroom last year.

2 🔊 1.31 **Listen again and repeat the sentences.**

3 **Underline the *schwa* sounds in the following sentences.**
  1 Mark is older than Julia, but Peter is the oldest in the class.
  2 The River Nile is longer than the River Danube.
  3 The weather is warmer in Spain than in England.

4 🔊 1.32 **Listen and check your answers.**

Unit 5 won't/want

1 🔊 2.03 **Listen and repeat.**
  1 won't   2 want

2 🔊 2.04 **Listen and choose the sentences you hear.**
  1 a They want to study Maths.
     b They won't study Maths.
  2 a I want to travel around the world.
     b I won't travel around the world.

Say it right!

3 🔊 **2.04** Listen again and repeat the sentences.

Unit 6 Contractions: *will*

1 🔊 **2.13** Listen and repeat.

1. I will → I'll
2. You will → You'll
3. He will → He'll
4. She will → She'll
5. We will → We'll
6. They will → They'll

2 🔊 **2.14** Listen and choose the option you hear.

1. I pass / I'll pass my driving test.
2. You like / You'll like this film.
3. They play / They'll play football for their country.
4. We study / We'll study together.
5. I go / I'll go to university.
6. We see / We'll see them at school.

3 Read the conversation and add in contractions of *will* in the correct place.

Kate:	Did you see Stuart this morning? He doesn't look very happy.
Paul:	He'll be OK. He's upset because he didn't pass his driving test.
Kate:	Oh well, he pass it next year. What about you? Do you think you take your test one day?
Paul:	I probably take it next year. If I pass, I buy a car.
Kate:	Lucky you! I think I be an old woman before I pass!
Paul:	We probably both be retired!

4 🔊 **2.15** Listen and check.

Unit 7 *have/has*

1 🔊 **2.26** Listen. Which sentence do you hear?

1. a It's stopped raining.
   b It stopped raining.
2. a My mum's read six books.
   b My mum read six books.
3. a I've started to learn English.
   b I started to learn English.

2 🔊 **2.26** Listen and repeat.

Unit 8 Word stress

1 Complete the table with the adjectives of feeling on page 88.

O	bored, …
oO	….
Oo	….
oOo	….
Ooo	….

2 🔊 **2.35** Listen, check and repeat.

Unit 6 Reading 1 p64

What do you want to be when you GROW UP?

Read the key below. Work with a partner. Do you agree with what the quiz says about you? Why/Why not?

How many As, Bs and Cs have you got?

Mostly As: You don't enjoy strange situations. You prefer planning things. Think about working in a library or an office.

Mostly Bs: You love helping animals and people. What about being a vet, a nurse, a dentist or a doctor?

Mostly Cs: You're obviously a creative person. We suggest you work as a writer, an artist, a musician, or an actor.

A mix: You like doing lots of different things but you also like being with people. How about being a teacher, a tour guide or a police officer?

Grammar reference

Starter Unit

Subject pronouns and *be*

+	I	am	
	He / She / It	is	13 years old.
	You / We / They	are	
–	I	'm not	
	He / She / It	isn't	from Manchester.
	You / We / They	aren't	
?	Am	I	
	Is	he / she / it	in a sports team?
	Are	you / we / they	

+	Yes,	I	am.
		he / she / it	is.
		you / we / they	are.
–	No,	I	'm not.
		he / she / it	isn't.
		you / we / they	aren't.

- *I, you, he, she, it, we,* and *they* are subject pronouns. We use them before the verb to say who does the action:
  I'm Nathan and I'm from Newcastle.
- We use *be* to describe people and things, say how old they are, where they are, where they are from etc:
  I'm John. I'm 14 years old. I'm from Scotland.

1 Write complete questions with *be*. Then write true answers for you. Use subject pronouns in your answers.

1. How old / you?
   How old are you? I'm 13 years old.
2. your best friend / in your class?
3. Where / your friends?
4. your pencil case / on your desk?
5. When / your next Maths class?
6. you and your friends / from Colombia?

Possessive *'s*

| singular | My brother's name is Matt. |
| plural | My friends' names are Kate, Lucy and Natalie. |

- We use the possessive *'s* to talk about our things or possessions:
  My sister's bike, my dad's car, etc (NOT *the bike of my sister*).
- With a plural noun, we write the apostrophe (') after the *s*:
  My friends' phones, my cousins' dog etc.

2 Write one sentence with possessive *'s*.

1. My sister's got a bike. It's blue.
   My sister's bike is blue.
2. My best friend's got a dog. It's very big.
3. My parents have got a car. It's new.
4. I've got three cousins. Their names are Jack, Will and Frances.
5. My teacher has got two cats. They're black.
6. My friends have got skateboards. They're under their desks.

there is/are, some/any

	singular	plural
+	There's some food on the floor.	There are some posters on the walls.
–	There isn't any milk on the table.	There aren't any students in the canteen.
?	Is there any water in your glass?	Are there any balls outside?

| + | Yes, there is. | Yes, there are. |
| – | No, there isn't. | No, there aren't. |

- We use *there is / are* to say something exists (or doesn't exist):
  There's a computer in my bedroom but there isn't a TV.
- We use *there is* with singular and uncountable nouns:
  There's a dog in the park.
- We use *there are* with plural countable nouns:
  There are 10 laptops in the IT room.
- We often use *there is / are* with *some* in affirmative sentences:
  There's some orange juice for you.
- We often use *there is / are* with *any* in negative sentences and questions:
  Are there any books on the floor?

3 Circle the correct words and then write *some* or *any*.

1. A *Is there / Are there* .... pencils under your desk?
   B No, *there isn't / there aren't* but *there is / there are* .... rubbers.
2. A *There isn't / There aren't* .... English dictionaries in the classroom.
   B Yes, I know but *there is / there are* two big dictionaries in the library.
3. A *Is there / Are there* .... orange juice?
   B No, *there isn't / there aren't* but *there is / there are* .... cola.
4. A *Is there / Are there* an IT room in your school?
   B No, *there isn't / there aren't* but *there is / there are* .... laptops in all the classrooms.

Grammar reference

have got

+	I / You / We / They	have got	an apple.
	He / She / It	has got	
–	I / You / We / They	haven't got	any cousins.
	He / She / It	hasn't got	
?	Have	I / you / we / they	a dog?
	Has	he / she / it	

+	Yes,	I / you / we / they	have.
		he / she / it	has.
–	No,	I / you / we / they	haven't.
		he / she / it	hasn't.

- We use *have / has got* to talk about our family, our hair or eyes and our possessions:
  I've got a sister. She's got brown hair and blue eyes.

4 Complete the sentences with *has got, have got, hasn't got* or *haven't got*.

1. I .... (✗) a big family. I .... (✓) a brother, a mum and a dad.
2. My mum .... (✓) three brothers but she .... (✗) any sisters.
3. .... you .... a rubber in your pencil case?
4. My best friend .... (✗) a skateboard but he .... (✓) a new mountain bike.
5. My friends .... (✓) PE now but I .... (✓) Maths.
6. What .... the teacher .... in that big bag?

Present simple: affirmative and negative

+	I / You / We / They	play	basketball.
	He / She / It	plays	
–	I / You / We / They	don't go	swimming.
	He / She / It	doesn't go	

- We use the present simple to talk about facts, habits and routines:
  I play football after school every day.

Spelling: third person

- With most verbs, we add *-s*:
  play – he plays   live – he lives
- With verbs that end in consonant + *-y*, remove the *-y* and add *-ies*:
  study – she studies   fly – it flies
- With verbs that end in *-o, -ss, -sh, -ch, -x* and *-zz*, add *-es*:
  *does   misses   washes   watches
  relaxes   buzzes*

5 Write sentences in the present simple.

1. In winter, I (✗ go skiing / ✓ go snowboarding).
   In winter, I don't go skiing. I go snowboarding.
2. My mum (✓ have lunch at work / ✗ have lunch at home).
3. My cousins (✗ live near me / ✓ live in Glasgow).
4. My best friend (✓ do his homework / ✗ watch TV).
5. My brother (✗ study French / ✓ study English).

Present simple: questions

?	Do	I / you / we / they	play	volleyball?
	Does	he / she / it		

+	Yes,	I / you / we / they	do.
		he / she / it	does.
–	No,	I / you / we / they	don't.
		he / she / it	doesn't.

6 Write questions in the present simple.

1. A: .... you .... basketball?
   B: No, I don't. I play football.
2. A: How often .... your sister .... swimming?
   B: She goes swimming every day.
3. A: .... your parents .... TV after dinner?
   B: Yes, they do. They always watch TV after dinner.
4. A: Where .... your best friend .... ?
   B: She lives near me.
5. A: When .... you and your friends .... skateboarding?
   B: We go skateboarding at the weekend.

Adverbs of frequency

always   usually   often   sometimes   never
100%   0%

- We use the present simple with **adverbs of frequency** to say how often we do things.
  I sometimes go snowboarding in the winter.
- With the verb *be*, we put the adverb after the verb:
  I'm often tired after playing football.
- With other verbs in the present simple, we put the adverb before the main verb:
  I sometimes go cycling with my friends.

7 Put the words in order to make sentences.

1. library / the / We / do / in / sometimes / English
2. work / dad / often / cycling / after / goes / My
3. always / is / brother / happy / My
4. lunch / canteen / usually / have / I / the / in
5. grandparents / never / skiing / My / go

Grammar reference

Unit 1

Present continuous

+	I	am	eating.
	He / She / It	is	
	You / We / They	are	
−	I	am not	
	He / She / It	isn't	
	You / We / They	aren't	
?	Am	I	eating?
	Is	he / she / it	
	Are	you / we / they	

+	Yes,	I	am.
		he / she / it	is.
		you / we / they	are.
−	No,	I	am not.
		he / she / it	isn't.
		you / we / they	aren't.

- We use the present continuous to talk about actions in progress at the time of speaking.
  You're reading the Grammar reference.

1 Complete the sentences with the present continuous form of the verb in brackets.
1. I …. (visit) an amazing shopping centre right now.
2. We …. (study) in the library today.
3. I can see Martha. She …. (not play) tennis. It's badminton.
4. What film …. you …. (watch) on TV? Is it good?
5. My parents are in the kitchen but they …. (not cook).
6. …. your friends …. (shop) in town at the moment? Yes, they …. .

Present simple vs. present continuous

- We use the present simple to talk about facts, habits and routines. We use adverbs of frequency with the present simple.
  I never go to the cinema.
- We use the present continuous to talk about actions in progress at the time of speaking. We use *at the moment* and *(right) now* with the present continuous.
  I am reading my emails at the moment.

2 Choose the correct words.
1. Paula **look / looks / is looking / are looking** at trainers in a sports shop right now.
2. Dan and Eddie **play / plays / is playing / are playing** rugby on Saturdays.
3. Where **do / does / am / are** you usually **go / goes / going / to go** after class?
4. **Do / Does / Is / Are** she **buy / buys / buying / to buy** a tablet right now?
5. We **eat / eats / am eating / are eating** at the shopping mall now.

(don't) want to, would(n't) like to, would prefer to

- *Would like* is more polite than *want*.
  I want to have pizza for dinner, please. (= child to parent)
  I'd like to have some chips with my fish, please. (= customer to waiter).
- We use *would prefer* to say what we want to do in a situation (not in general).
  I would prefer to buy my new trainers in the sports shop.
- We use the infinitive with *to* after *want*, *would like* and *would prefer*.
  She'd like to see the new shopping centre.

3 Write sentences or questions.
1. I / would like / visit / the zoo
2. My brother / not want / go / to the theme park
3. We / would prefer / watch / a funny film
4. your cousin / want / sell / his old games console?
5. My friends / not would like / live / in another town
6. Would like / you / have / dinner with us?

(not) enough + noun

- We use *enough* + noun to say we've got what we need or want.
  I can buy a new mobile phone. I've got enough money.
- We use *not enough* + noun to say we've got less than we need or want.
  I can't buy a new phone. I haven't got enough money.
- *Enough* goes before the noun.
  We can't make a cake. There isn't enough milk.

4 Order the words to make sentences.
1. money / tablet / enough / haven't / for / a / I / got
2. you / got / time / help / enough / Have / me / to / ?
3. are / enough / for / There / oranges / orange juice
4. enough / We / got / haven't / for / chairs / everyone
5. car / Our / enough / isn't / six / people / for / big

100 Grammar reference

Grammar reference

Unit 2

was/were: affirmative and negative

+	I / He / She / It	was	calm.
	You / We / They	were	
−	I / He / She / It	wasn't	
	You / We / They	weren't	

Was and were are the past simple forms of be.
He was a tennis player. They weren't actors.

1 Complete the sentences with was, were, wasn't or weren't.
1. My friends .... tired after the match.
2. You .... late for school yesterday.
3. We .... (not) in class at 7 o'clock.
4. I .... born in 2002.
5. Nelson Mandela .... (not) from England.
6. It .... (not) cold last night.

Past simple: affirmative, negative and time expressions

+	I / You / He / She / It / We / They	watched TV last night.
−		didn't play tennis on Thursday.

- We use the past simple to talk about completed events and actions in the past.
  We played basketball yesterday.
- We often use time expressions such as *yesterday, last week, at 6 o'clock, in 2007, on Monday,* etc. with the past simple to say when the action happened.
  My parents weren't at work at 6 o'clock.

Past Simple: spelling

- For verbs ending in -e, we add -d.
  like – liked   live – lived
- For verbs ending in consonant + -y, we remove the -y and add -ied.
  copy – copied   study – studied   bully – bullied
- For verbs ending in consonant + vowel + consonant, we double the last consonant and add -ed.
  *shop – shopped   stop – stopped
  travel – travelled*
- Some verbs are irregular in the past simple. They don't follow any pattern.
- See the irregular verb list on p127.

2 Write sentences in the past simple.
1. Marie Curie / live / in Paris.
2. My dad / fly / to New York five days ago.
3. My friends / not play / football in the morning.
4. I / win / a race at school yesterday.
5. We / not buy / anything at the shopping centre on Saturday.
6. My sister / find / some money on the floor.

was/were: questions and short answers

?	Was	I / he / she / it	friendly?
	Were	you / we / they	
+	Yes,	I / he / she / it	was.
		you / we / they	were.
−	No,	I / he / she / it	wasn't.
		you / we / they	weren't.

3 Write questions with the past simple of the verb be.
1. Where / she / born?
2. What / her first film?
3. What / her favourite subjects at school?
4. you / interested in acting / at school?
5. your father / a film director?
6. your parents / interested in films?

Past simple: questions and short answers

?	Did	I / you / he / she / it / we / they	sleep?
+	Yes,	I / you / he / she / it / we / they	did.
−	No,		didn't.

4 Read the answers and write questions in the past simple.
1. A: Where .... last night?
   B: I went to the cinema.
2. A: Who .... at the restaurant?
   B: I saw a famous actor.
3. A: When .... on holiday?
   B: My parents went on holiday a week ago.
4. A: .... at the concert last night?
   B: No, I wasn't at the concert. I was at home.
5. A: .... for the exam after school?
   B: Yes, I did. I studied for two hours.
6. A: Why .... about your grandmother?
   B: I wrote about her because I admire her.

Grammar reference

Unit 3

Past continuous: affirmative and negative

+	I / He / She / It	was	eating.
	You / We / They	were	
−	I / He / She / It	wasn't	
	You / We / They	weren't	

- We use the past continuous to talk about a long action in progress at a certain time in the past.
  At midday, I was having lunch with my friend.

1 Write sentences in the past continuous.
At 5 o'clock yesterday afternoon ...
1 My teacher (✗ read / ✓ talk to a friend).
   My teacher wasn't reading. She was talking to a friend.
2 The dog (✗ sleep / ✓ run in the garden).
3 I (✗ write a letter / ✓ read an email).
4 The children (✗ watch TV / ✓ do homework).
5 You (✗ study / ✓ play computer games).
6 It (✗ rain / ✓ snow).

Past continuous: questions and short answers

?	Were	you / they / we	walking?
	Was	he / she / it / I	

+	Yes,	you / they / we	were.
		he / she / it / I	was.
−	No,	you / they / we	weren't.
		he / she / it / I	wasn't.

2 Complete the questions and answers with the past continuous.
1 A: What .... you .... (do) last night?
   B: I .... (listen) to music, but I .... (not listen) to it loudly.
2 A: .... Rachel .... (watch) a film this afternoon?
   B: No, she ..... She .... (tidy) her bedroom.
3 A: Where .... they .... (chase) the dog?
   B: They .... (chase) it in the park, but they .... (not run) very fast.
4 A: .... you .... (study) for the Science test yesterday?
   B: Yes, I ..... I .... (work) with Ben.

Past simple vs. continuous

- We use the past continuous to talk about a long action that was in progress in the past. We use the past simple to talk about a short action that interrupts another long action. We usually use *when* before the past simple and *while* before the past continuous.
  I was talking to my mum when I heard the news.

3 Complete the sentences with the past simple or past continuous form of the verb in brackets.
1 I .... (break) my arm while I .... (climb) a tree.
2 Dan .... (do) a Maths test, when his phone .... (ring).
3 The police .... (catch) the thief while he .... (jump) over the wall.
4 When my mum .... (get) home, we .... (not do) our homework.
5 While I .... (take) photos in the town centre, I .... (see) my best friend.
6 My friends .... (swim) in the sea when it .... (start) to rain.

could/couldn't: affirmative, negative, questions and short answers

+	I / You / He / She / It / We / They	could	swim very well.
−		couldn't	

?	Could	I / you / he / she / it / we / they	swim very well?

+	Yes,	I / you / he / she / it / we / they	could.
−	No,		couldn't.

- We use *could/couldn't* to talk about ability and possibility in the past.
  When I was five, I could swim 20 metres.

4 Complete the sentences with *could(n't)* and the verb in brackets.
1 I .... when I was five. (read)
2 She .... very fast because she was tired. (not run)
3 Sam .... the board because he wasn't wearing his glasses. (not see)
4 .... the piano when he was small? (Tony, play)
5 We .... him because he spoke slowly. (understand)
6 .... a bike when you were a child? (you, ride)

Grammar reference

Unit 4

Comparatives and superlatives

	Adjective	Comparative	Superlative
Short adjectives	high	add -er: higher	add -est: the highest
Short adjectives ending vowel + consonant	big	double the final consonant and add -er: bigger	double the final consonant and add -est: the biggest
Adjectives ending -y	tidy	remove the -y and add -ier: tidier	remove the -y and add -iest: the tidiest
Long adjectives	comfortable	more comfortable	the most comfortable
Irregular adjectives	good	better	the best

- We use comparative adjectives to compare one thing with another. Use the verb + a comparative adjective + *than*.
  My room is tidier than my sister's room.
- We use superlative adjectives to say that one thing or person has got the most of a particular quality. Use *the* with a superlative adjective.
  My parents have got the biggest bedroom.

1 Complete the sentences with the comparative or superlative form of the adjective or adverb.
1 My bedroom is .... my sister's room. (small)
2 We stayed at .... hotel in the city. (bad)
3 I run .... my brother. (fast)
4 We all eat fast in my family, but my older brother eats .... . (quickly)
5 Scott is .... player on the team. (good)
6 I think doing housework is .... doing homework. (boring)

must and mustn't

+	I / You / He / She / It / We / They	must	speak.
–		mustn't	

- We use *must* to talk about obligation or strong recommendations.
  We must do our homework.
- We use *mustn't* to talk about prohibition and strong advice against something.
  They mustn't talk in the cinema.

2 Complete the sentences with *must* or *mustn't* and the verb in brackets.
1 Children .... (go) to school.
2 You .... (wear) a helmet when you ride a motorbike.
3 You .... (swim) on a beach when the flag is red.
4 You .... (talk) in a library.
5 When the traffic lights are red, you .... (stop).
6 You .... (forget) your passport when you travel to another country.

should and shouldn't

+	I / You / He / She / It / We / They	should	be quiet.
–		shouldn't	

?	Should	I / you / he / she / it / we / they	go out?

+	Yes,	I / you / he / she / it / we / they	should.
–	No,		shouldn't.

- We use *should* and *shouldn't* when we give advice or recommendations.
  You should study for the exam.

3 Complete the questions with *should* and the words in brackets. Then answer the questions.
1 A: I'm bored. Who <u>should I phone</u> ? (I / phone)
   B: <u>You should phone a friend. You shouldn't phone your teacher.</u>
2 A: We're hungry but lunch is in 30 minutes. What .... ? (we / eat)
   B: ....
3 A: My brother's got an exam tomorrow. What time .... ? (he / go to bed)
   B: ....
4 A: I would like to visit your town. When .... ? (I / visit)
   B: ....
5 A: My friends want to try a new sport. What .... ? (they / try)
   B: ....
6 A: My sister wants to learn French. Where .... ? (she / go)
   B: ....

Grammar reference

Unit 5

will/won't

+ −	I / You / He / She / It / We / They	will	work.
		won't	

?	Will	I / you / he / she / it / we / they	go?

+ −	Yes, No,	I / you / he / she / it / we / they	will. won't.

- We use *will* and *won't* to make predictions about the future.
  Computers will control our lives in the future.
- In informal English we can use the contraction *'ll*. We don't use *'ll* in short answers.
  A: *I'll go to university.*
  B: *Will you go to university in the UK?*
  A: *Yes, I will.*
- We use an infinitive without *to* after *will* and *won't*.
  They will do their homework on a tablet.
  (*They will to do their homework on a tablet.*)

1 Complete the sentences with *will* or *won't* and the verb in brackets.

1 Where …. you …. (live) in the future?
2 Computers …. (be) faster in five years.
3 We …. (not buy) big phones in the future.
4 …. Ella …. (study) computer science?
5 Most people …. (not use) keyboards in a few years.
6 You …. (need) Wi-Fi in your new home.

may/might

+ −	I / You / He / She / It / We / They	may / might	work.
		may not / might not	

?	May / Might	I / you / he / she / it / we / they	go?

+ −	Yes, No,	I / you / he / she / it / we / they	may /might. may not / might not.

- We use *may* and *might* to say that it is possible (but not certain) that something will happen in the future:
  It may / might rain later. (It's possible)
- Like *will / won't* (see above), *may* and *might* don't change in the different persons and we use an infinitive without *to* after them:
  My brother may study in Paris or he might go to London. (*he might to go to London*)

2 Choose the correct words.

1 I'm sure I **will** / **may** watch the film.
2 My teacher **will** / **might** give us a lot of homework. That's certain.
3 We **may** / **will** go to Prague or we **might** / **will** go to Budapest. We aren't sure.
4 That exam was difficult. I'm sure I **won't** / **might not** pass.
5 I **will** / **may** become a famous scientist. It's possible!
6 My friends **won't** / **may not** go to the cinema. They aren't certain.

First conditional

action/situation (*if-*)	result
If we **buy** this laptop,	we'll **get** a free printer.
result	**action/situation (*if-*)**
He'll **use** your email	if you **tell** him the password.

- We use the first conditional to talk about the future result of an action or situation.
  If the tablet breaks, I will take it to the shop.
- There are two clauses/parts in conditional sentences; an if clause and a result clause. We use *if* + subject + present simple to talk about the action or situation. We use subject + *will* + infinitive without *to* to talk about the result. We put a comma after the if-clause.
  If we pass all our exams, we'll have a party.

3 Write sentences in the first conditional with the phrases in the box.

main clause	result
1 I / walk / to school	I / be / late
2 John / buy / a computer	he / read / many books
3 you / scroll down	you / see / an amazing photo
4 Mia and Sara / watch / TV all evening	they / finish / their homework
5 we / turn down / the music	we / hear the singer
6 my parents / get / a new laptop	you / see / an amazing photo

1 *If I walk, to school, I will be late.*

Grammar reference

Unit 6

be going to: affirmative, negative, questions and short answers

+	I	am		
	He / She / It	is		
	You / We / They	are	going to	work.
−	I	am not		
	He / She / It	isn't		
	You / We / They	aren't		

?	Am	I		
	Is	he / she / it	going to	work?
	Are	you / we / they		

+ Yes,	I	am.
	he / she / it	is.
	you / we / they	are.
− No,	I	'm not.
	he / she / it	isn't.
	you / we / they	aren't.

- We use *be going to* to talk about future plans and intentions.
  I'm going to work in another country in the future.
- We form the affirmative with *be + going to +* infinitive.
  They're going to leave school this year.
- We form the negative with *be + not + going to +* infinitive.
  He isn't going to take a year out.
- We form questions with *be* before the subject.
  Are they going to get married this year?
- We form information questions with *Wh-* question word before *be*.
  What is she going to study at university?

1 Complete the sentences with the correct form of *be going to* and the verbs in brackets.

1 We …. (not play) tennis after school today.
2 …. you …. (get married) when you're older?
3 I …. (not leave) school until I'm 18.
4 My friends …. (have) a party next week.
5 My cousin …. (learn) to drive next summer.
6 Where …. your brother …. (stay) when he goes to Australia?

will vs. *be going to*

- We use *will* for predictions:
  You'll pass all your exams, I'm sure.
- We can also use *will* when we make a decision just before we speak.
  A: Let's have a party!
  B: That's a good idea! I'll send everyone a message.
  or when we offer to help someone:
  A: It's mum's birthday. I don't know what to buy her.
  B: Don't worry. I'll go shopping with you later.
- We use *going to* for plans or intentions:
  This summer, we're going to visit Moscow.

2 Choose the correct words.

1 Those books are heavy. I **'ll / 'm going to** carry them.
2 My mum **will / 's going to** start working in my school next week.
3 I'm cold. I know, I **'ll / 'm going to** make you some hot chocolate.
4 My cousin **will / 's going to** have a baby next month.
5 We **won't / aren't going to** go on holiday this year.
6 My teacher thinks we **won't / aren't going to** need pens or pencils in the future.

Present continuous for the future

- We can use the present continuous to talk about definite plans and arrangements in the future.
  She's meeting her friends after school.
- We often use future time expressions such as *tonight, tomorrow, this weekend, this summer, next week, next month,* and *after class/school.*
  We're having dinner in a restaurant tonight.

3 Look at the diary. Then write sentences in the present continuous.

	Morning	Afternoon
Today		have a guitar lesson
Friday	do an exam	go to Harry's party
Saturday	play basketball	eat at Mario's Pizza
Sunday	visit our grandparents	

1 Tomorrow morning, I*'m doing an exam* .
2 This afternoon, I …. .
3 On Sunday morning, we …. .
4 I …. on Saturday morning.
5 On Friday afternoon, Harry …. .
6 My friends and I …. on Saturday afternoon.

Grammar reference

Unit 7

Present perfect: affirmative and negative

+	I / We / You / They	have	
	He / She / It	has	been.
−	I / We / You / They	haven't	
	He / She / It	hasn't	

- We use the present perfect to talk about events and experiences that happened at any time in the past.
  I've visited a lot of countries.

Spelling: past participles

- With regular verbs, we add *-ed* to the infinitive.
  crash – crashed   ask – asked
- With verbs ending in *-e* we add *-d*.
  like – liked   love – loved
- With verbs ending in consonant + *-y*, we remove the *-y* and add *-ied*.
  tidy – tidied   carry – carried
- With verbs ending in consonant + vowel + consonant, we double the final consonant and add *-ed*.
  slip – slipped   drop – dropped
- Some verbs have irregular past participle forms. They don't follow any pattern.
  cut – cut   fall – fallen
- See the irregular verb list on page 127.

1 Complete the sentences with the present perfect form of the verb in brackets.
1. Max .... (cut) his finger again.
2. They .... (crash) their car twice.
3. I .... (not see) a large snake before.
4. We .... (meet) lots of interesting people.
5. Frances .... (have) a very exciting holiday.
6. She .... (not burn) her hand.

Present perfect: questions

| ? | Have | I / we / you / they | eaten? |
| | Has | he / she / it | |

+	Yes,	I / we / you / they	have.
		he / she / it	has.
−	No,	I / we / you / they	haven't.
		he / she / it	hasn't.

- We use questions in the present perfect to ask about past experiences. We can use *ever* to ask about your whole life.
  Has she ever won a competition?

2 Write questions and short answers with the present perfect and *ever*.
1. you / have an accident ?
   Have you ever had an accident?
   No, ...
2. Louisa / fall off her bike ?
   Yes, ...
3. Tim / hurt his wrist ?
   No, ...
4. your parents / live in Africa ?
   No, ...
5. your best friend / lose something important ?
   Yes, ...
6. your friends / win a sports competition ?
   No, ...

Past simple vs. present perfect

- We use the past simple to say when something happened. We use words like *last week*, *yesterday*, *two weeks ago* with the past simple.
  I broke my foot last weekend.
- We use the present perfect when it's not important or we don't know when something happened. We use words like *ever*, *never*, *in the last ten years*, *in my life*, etc. with the present perfect.
  Have you ever broken something?
  No, I've never broken anything.

3 Choose the correct words.
1. Have you ever .... a snake?
   a eat   b ate   c eaten
2. Elsa .... some interesting things at the museum yesterday.
   a saw   b has seen   c see
3. .... you snowboard in the mountains when you went on holiday?
   a Do   b Did   c Have
4. What bones .... you broken?
   a did   b has   c have
5. I .... forgotten my mum's birthday.
   a did never   b have never   c do never
6. .... that new adventure film last week?
   a Did you see   b Have you seen   c Do you see

Grammar reference

Unit 8

one/ones

- We use *one/ones* to refer to a person or thing when we don't want to repeat a noun in a sentence. We use *one* in the singular and *ones* in the plural.
  I like all my presents, but this one is my favourite.
  A: Which birthday cards do you prefer?
  B: The cheapest ones.

1 Complete the conversations with *one* or *ones*.
1. A: Which trainers would you like, green or blue?
   B: I'd like the blue …. , please.
2. A: Which restaurant are you going to for your birthday?
   B: The …. next to the park.
3. A: What kind of ticket do you want?
   B: Which …. is the cheapest?
4. A: I really like playing those computer games.
   B: Which …. ?
   A: Football games.
5. A: Which photos do you like best?
   B: I'm not sure. Perhaps the …. with children and animals.
6. A: Do you want to go to the same swimming pool?
   B: No, I'd like to try a different …. , please.

Indefinite pronouns

	People	Things	Places
+	someone everyone	something everything	somewhere everywhere
−	no one anyone	nothing anything	nowhere anywhere

- We use indefinite pronouns to refer to people, things and places in a general way.
  I want to go somewhere at the weekend.
- These words are singular.
  Everyone is excited about the wedding.
- We usually use an affirmative verb with *no one*, *nothing* and *nowhere*.
  There's nothing to do here!
- We usually use a negative verb with *anyone*, *anything* and *anywhere*.
  I haven't got anything to do today.

2 Complete the sentences with the words in the box.

| anywhere   Everyone   nothing |
| Someone   anything   something |

1. I haven't got …. to do today.
2. Helen couldn't find her keys …. .
3. …. called me on the phone but I don't know who.
4. I'm so hungry. I've eaten …. all day.
5. If you're bored, I can give you …. to do.
6. …. is going to the park tomorrow. Why don't you come, too?

too + adjective

- We often use *too* + *adjective* to say something is more than we want or need.
  The dog's too big to sit on that chair.
- *Too* goes before the adjective.
  We're too tired to walk.
- We can use *to* + infinitive after *too* + adjective.
  It's too cold to swim in the lake.

(not) adjective + enough

| + | My sister can take my dad's car. She's old enough to drive. |
| − | Can you write the date on the board? I'm not tall enough to write at the top. |

- We often use (*not*) adjective + *enough* to say something is less than we want or need.
  I'm not old enough to see that film.
- *Enough* goes after the adjective.
  It isn't cold enough to snow. (*It isn't enough cold…*)
- We can use *to* + infinitive after (*not*) adjective *enough*.
  It isn't warm enough to go swimming.
  (*It isn't warm enough for going…*)

3 Complete the sentences with *too* + adjective or (*not*) adjective + *enough*. Use the adjectives in brackets.
1. The tree is …. to climb. (high)
2. My friends are …. to see that film. You must be 18. (old)
3. I'm …. to see the band from here. Can we go over there? (tall)
4. This coffee is …. to drink at the moment. (hot)
5. My team is …. to win this match but we'll try very hard. (good)
6. The bus is …. to get us to school on time. We're going to be late! (slow)

Vocabulary Bank

Jog your memory!

1 Cover the rest of the page. How many shops and money verbs can you remember?

Shops

bookshop	electronics shop	shoe shop
chemist	music shop	sports shop
clothes shop	newsagent	supermarket
department store		

1 Think of two things you can buy from each shop in the box.

bookshop – magazine, dictionary

2 Work with a partner. Say two things you can buy in one of the shops. Your partner says the shop. Then swap.

Money verbs

spend   buy   sell   borrow   save   earn

1 Which four verbs in the box often go with the word *money*? Which two verbs often go with things like *clothes, shoes, books*, etc.?

2 Write true sentences about you with the words.

1 I sometimes spend money in the music shop.

Explore *extreme adjectives*

~~amazing~~	brilliant	huge	terrible
awful	freezing	horrible	wonderful
boiling	great		

1 Complete the table with the words in the box.

very good	very bad	other
amazing		

2 Work with a partner. Decide together on things which are *amazing, awful, brilliant*, etc.

The Dubai shopping mall is amazing.

Explore prefixes

afraid	happy	lucky	usual
clear	important	tidy	well
friendly	interesting		

1 What do we add to the adjectives in the box to make the negative?

2 Work with a partner. Think of a situation for six of the negative adjectives.

When you are ill, you feel unwell.

Shops and money
bookshop (n)

Study tip

Start a vocabulary notebook or make some vocabulary cards. Keep a record of all your new words. Write the heading '*Shops and money*' and write the words on this page under this heading. Don't forget to write the part of speech next to the new word, e.g. *noun*, *verb* or *adjective*.

Vocabulary Bank

UNIT 2

🧠 Jog your memory!

1 Cover the rest of the page. How many jobs and adjectives of character can you remember?

Jobs

actor	firefighter	scientist
artist	police officer	vet
astronaut	musician	
dancer	nurse	

1 Look at the words in the box. What do the people do?
An actor acts in films or plays.

2 Work with a partner. Say what one of the people does. Your partner says the job. Then swap.

🔍 Explore expressions with *make*

a bed	history	a suggestion
a cake	mistakes	sure
friends	a phone call	

1 Look at the words in the box for one minute. Cover them. How many can you remember?

2 Work with a partner. Write true/false sentences about you with the phrases.
Yesterday, I made a cake.

3 Tell your partner your sentences. He/She must guess if they are true or false.

Adjectives of character

brave	friendly	quiet
calm	funny	serious
cheerful	kind	

1 Match the words in the box with some of the jobs on this page and write a sentence. Compare your sentences with a partner.
An actor needs to be brave and funny.

🔍 Explore the suffix *-ness*

friendly	kind	tidy
happy	quiet	weak
ill	sad	

1 Look at the words in the box. What do we add to these adjectives to make nouns? Write down the nouns but check your spelling!

2 Work with a partner. Say the noun. Your partner makes a sentence with the adjective. Then swap.

📝 Study tip

Actor – an actor acts in films and plays.

Write a short definition of the words in your vocabulary notebook or on the cards. This will help you to remember the meaning. When you study these words later, cover the word, read your definition and try to remember the word.

Vocabulary Bank

Jog your memory!

1. Cover the rest of the page. How many action verbs and adverbs of manner can you remember?

Action verbs

catch	fall over	run
chase	hide	throw
climb	jump	

1. Work with a partner. Look at the words in the box. Choose a verb. Don't tell your partner. Draw a picture. Can your partner guess which verb it is?

Adverbs of manner

| badly | easily | quietly | quickly |
| carefully | happily | slowly | well |

1. Look at the words in the box for one minute. Close your books and write down the eight adverbs. Then open your books and check your spelling.

2. Work with a partner. Think of some things you do every day, e.g. *get up, have breakfast, walk to school,* etc. Then write sentences with these things and the adverbs.
   We have breakfast quickly and we walk to school slowly.

Explore expressions

1. Complete the questions with a verb and the prepositions in the box. The same verb is missing in each one. What is it?

   | up   through   after   like   out   for |

   1. Do you ever have to …. …. younger brothers, sisters or cousins? When?
   2. How often do you …. …. your homework carefully before you give it to your teacher?
   3. If you can't find your mobile phone, where do you …. …. it?
   4. Who do you …. …. in your family?
   5. When was the last time you shouted '…. …. !' at someone? What happened?
   6. If you don't know the meaning of a word, do you …. it …. in a dictionary?

2. Work with a partner. Ask and answer the questions in Exercise 1.

Explore nouns with -er

| build | farm | photograph | swim |
| explore | island | shop | paint |

1. Write nouns with *-er* using the words in the box above.

2. Add more nouns with *-er* to your list.

3. Draw a picture of one of your words. Your partner must guess the word. Then swap.

Study tip

If it's difficult to think of a definition for the new words in your vocabulary notebook or on your cards, then draw a picture to help you remember the meaning.

Vocabulary Bank

UNIT 4

🧠 Jog your memory!

1 Cover the rest of the page. How many things in the home and household appliances can you remember?

Things in the home

| blanket | cupboard | desk | mirror | towel |
| carpet | curtains | pillow | shelf | wardrobe |

1 Write the words from the box in the correct column. Some words can go in more than one column.

bedroom	bathroom	living room	kitchen
blanket			

2 Add two more new words to each column.

Household appliances

cooker	fridge	iron
dishwasher	hairdryer	lamp
freezer	heater	washing machine

1 Look at the words for one minute. Then close your book. Write down the household appliances. Open your book and check your spelling. How many are correct?

2 Write down the household appliances in order of the most useful to least useful.

3 Compare your list with a partner.

🔍 Explore expressions with *do*

| the washing | the ironing | sports | homework |
| housework | the washing | Maths | |

1 Look at the words in the box. Which of the things do you enjoy/not enjoy doing? Think of some more words to add to the list.

2 Write five sentences about you and the people you know. Use *do* and five of the words in the box.

3 Work with a partner. Don't show him/her your sentences. Read your sentence without the word(s) after *do*. Can your partner guess the word(s)?

🔍 Explore verbs with *up* or *down*

| go up / down | put up / down |
| get / come up | sit down / stand up |

1 Complete the sentences with the correct form of some of the verbs in the box.
1 I usually .... in the morning when the sun .....
2 We always .... when the teacher comes in the classroom. We can .... when she tells us.
3 I'm going to .... some pictures on my wall.
4 It takes a lot longer to .... the hill on a bicycle than it does to .... it.
5 .... your pens and listen.

2 Work with a partner. Think of more verbs with *up* or *down*. (think of verbs of movement e.g. walk, climb, etc.). Write sentences with the verbs.

cupboard → p silent

📝 Study tip

When you write down a word, make sure you spell it correctly. Then, when you learn the word, remember to learn the correct spelling too!

Vocabulary Bank

🧠 Jog your memory!

1 Cover the rest of the page. How many computer words and technology verbs + prepositions can you remember?

Computer words

keyboard	microchip	smartphone
laptop	mouse	tablet
memory stick	printer	touchscreen

Technology verbs + prepositions

Click on the icon.	Sign into your account.
Log onto your computer.	Turn down the volume.
Scroll down the webpage.	Turn on the laptop.
Shut down the computer.	Turn up the volume.

1 Look at the words in the box. Which of the things can we …?
- hold in one hand?
- connect to a computer?
- use instead of a computer?
- find on or inside a computer?

2 Work with a partner. Which of these things do you have in your house? How often do you use them?

1 Look at the words in the box. Write true sentences for five verbs.
I always turn on my laptop when I get home.

2 Work with a partner. Mime one of the sentences. Your partner must guess the technology verb.

🔍 Explore suffixes *-ful* and *-less*

beauty	colour	power	use	
care	pain	success	wonder	

1 We can use *-ful* with all of the words in the box to make adjectives but we can only add *-less* to five of these words. Which ones?

2 Read the sentences. What's the difference between *hopeful* and *hopeless*?
I studied really hard for the exam and it wasn't very difficult. I'm **hopeful** that I'll do well.
I'm really bad at throwing and catching balls. I'm **hopeless** at basketball.

🔍 Explore phrasal verbs 1

get up	look for	take off	wake up
go back	put on	turn on	

1 Think about what you usually do on a school day. Write some sentences with the phrasal verbs from the box in the same order as you do them.
I wake up at 7 am and then I get up.

2 Work with a partner. Compare your sentences. Do you do the same things every day? Do you do them in the same order?
Do you put on your clothes before you turn on the TV?

> turn on (v) I always turn on my laptop when I get home.

📝 Study tip

If you can't think of a definition, write an example sentence next to your new words. Try to write an interesting sentence. Remember, if this example sentence is about you or people you know, you will remember the word more easily.

Vocabulary Bank

UNIT 6

🧠 Jog your memory!

1 Cover the rest of the page. How many life events and containers and materials can you remember?

Life events

be born	learn to drive
get a job	leave home
get married	leave school
go to university	start school
have children	take a year out

1 Look at the words in the box. Which of these things do we usually do …?
- before we're 6 years old?
- before we're 20?
- before we're 30?
- after we're 30?

2 Work with a partner. Add some more life events to the list.
buy a car or a house

Containers and materials

bag	jars	bottles
cartons	cans	
cardboard box	crisp packet	

1 Write the containers from the box in the correct column. Some can go in more than one column.

paper	plastic	glass	metal
bag	*bag*		

2 Work with a partner. Cover the words and test each other.
A: *What are bags made of?*
B: *Bags are made of paper or plastic.*

3 Work with a partner. Which of the containers do you often use? What for?

🔍 Explore phrasal verbs 2

find out	grow up	try on
get on / off	switch on / off	write down
go out	look for	

1 We do not usually use a noun after *go out* or *grow up*. Write at least two nouns for the other verbs in the box.

2 Write a question with five of the phrasal verbs.

3 Work with a partner. Ask and answer your questions.

🔍 Explore verbs with prepositions

agree	dream	spend (money)	wait
ask	learn	pay	
belong	listen	talk	

1 Which of the prepositions below do we use with each of the verbs in the box above?

| on   for (x2)   with   to (x4)   about (x2) |

agree with

2 Work with a partner. When did you last do the things in the box?

> listen (v) to: We need to listen to the teacher in class.

📝 Study tip

We need to use a preposition after some verbs. When you write down these verbs, always write down the preposition next to it. Don't forget to write an example sentence with the preposition too!

Vocabulary Bank

Jog your memory!

1 Cover the rest of the page. How many accidents and injuries and parts of the body can you remember?

Accidents and injuries

bang	fall off
break	hurt
burn	slip
crash	trap
cut	trip over

on ice	your finger
the dog	your hand
your back	your head
your bike	your leg
your car	

1 Match one word from each box to make accident and injury expressions.

2 Check your answers on page 75. Close your books. Say a verb. Your partner says the noun.

The body

ankle	elbow	shoulder	chest
back	knee	wrist	neck

1 Which parts of the body do people most often …?
   cut?   hurt?   burn?
   break?   bang?

2 Can you add some more parts of the body to the list?

Explore expressions with *get*

get better	get home	get sick
get dressed	get injured	get worried
get dark	get married	
get fit	get older	

1 Write sentences with five of the expressions.

2 Read a sentence to your partner without the expression. Can your partner guess the expression?

> Every morning, I have a shower and then I …

> Is it 'get dressed'?

Explore compound nouns

charity workers	forest floor
fishing boat	wildlife
firewood	

1 Look at the words in the box. Which of the words means …?
   - wood that you use to make a fire.
   - a boat that you use when you go fishing.
   - people who work for a charity.
   - the ground in the forest.
   - the animals, birds and plants that live in an area.

firewood, forest floor

Study tip

Remember to look at the words in this Vocabulary bank again and to try to learn them. If possible, work with a friend and test each other. Student A reads a definition or an example sentence without the word and Student B says the word.

Vocabulary Bank

UNIT 8

Jog your memory!

1 Cover the rest of the page. How many free time activities and adjectives of feeling can you remember?

Free time activities

draw pictures	read books or magazines
have a party	spend time with your family
meet friends	take photos
play an instrument	use the Internet
play computer games	watch films

1 Look at the words in the box. Write the words in order of your favourite to your least favourite.

2 Compare your list with your partner. Do you enjoy doing the same kinds of things?

Adjectives of feeling

afraid	bored	~~excited~~	surprised
upset	angry	embarrassed	interested
tired			

1 Look at the words in the box. Write them in the correct column.

😃	😐	😞
excited		

2 Choose one of the words but don't tell your partner. Mime the word. Can your partner guess what words it is?

Explore expressions

a good time	a rest	a meal
a shower	a problem	a party

1 Which verb goes with the words in the box?

2 Add the following words to the correct column.

sure	housework	a party	a bed	fun	
homework	a favour	a cake	a swim		
a suggestion	shopping				

make	do	have
sure	housework	a party

Explore making nouns from verbs

1 Look at these verbs. Write the noun.

have a party	_having a party_		
meet friend	….	take photos	….
play an instrument	….	use the Internet	….
play joke	….	watch films	….
read books	….		

2 Make nouns from verbs and write true and false sentences for you.
   I think meeting friends is boring.

3 Work with a partner. Guess which of your partner's sentences are true and false.

Study tip

Try to use your new vocabulary as soon as you can. This will help you to learn the new words and it will also help improve both your writing and speaking.

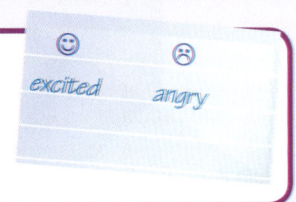

😃	😞
excited	angry

Vocabulary Bank 115

1 CLIL

Maths Percentages

1 Work with a partner. Match the symbols in the table with the words in the box.

> minus   divide   plus   per cent
> equals   multiply (by) / times

symbol	+	−	×	÷	%	=
name	1 …	2 …	3 …	4 …	5 …	6 …

2 🔊 1.37 Read and listen to the text. Which symbols from Exercise 1 do you use to calculate a percentage?

3 Read the text again and answer the questions.
1. Where does the word 'per cent' come from?
2. Who first used the numbers 0-9?
3. Why do we use percentages?
4. What percentage is 'the whole' equal to?
5. What is the whole in the example with cakes?
6. What do we multiply the fraction by to get the final percentage?

Your turn

4 Work with a partner. Calculate the percentage of chocolates that each person eats. Use the text to help you. The box has 60 chocolates.

	Chocolates	Percentage of whole box
James	12	1 ….
Susan	6	2 ….
Ahmed	15	3 ….
Susie	20	4 ….

PERCENTAGES

The word 'per cent' comes from Roman times. It comes from the Latin words *per centum* or 'out of 100'. Before the Romans, the ancient Egyptians used a similar system of numbers in tens. But the numbers from 0 to 9 that we use today come from the ancient Arab world, over 2,000 years ago. The Arabs also used fractions, for example, ¼ . We use percentages to calculate how much a part of a whole is. And when we say 'per cent', we're really saying 'out of 100'.

50% OF THIS BOX IS BLUE (50 OUT OF 100)

25% OF THIS BOX IS (25 OUT OF 100)

When we calculate a percentage of something, first we need to know the total number of things, or 'the whole'. The whole is 100%. For example, there are 12 cakes on a table. In this calculation, 12 is the whole and is 100%.

Next, we need to know the number we want to change to a percentage. For example, Tanya eats three of the cakes on the table so three is the number we want to change to a percentage.

We put these two numbers into a fraction. In our example, we need to calculate what percent three (number of cakes Tanya ate) is of twelve (total number of cakes). The fraction is 3/12. 3 ÷ 12 = 0.25.

Finally, we multiply this number by 100 to make a percentage. 0.25 × 100 = 25.

So Tanya ate 25% of the cakes.

Find out about our number system.

Discovery EDUCATION

1.4 What does Zero mean?

CLIL

History The feudal system

1 Match the words in the box with the pictures.

> knight   noble   peasants   king

2 🔊 1.38 Read and listen to the text. Complete the article with the people in Exercise 1.

3 Choose the correct answers.
1. The king gave his land to nobles **to sell / to look after**.
2. When a king died, **his son / the noble** inherited the fief.
3. Nobles helped the king **in battles / find more land**.
4. Knights were **never / sometimes** women.
5. Peasants were **at the bottom / in the middle** of the feudal system.
6. Peasants paid taxes to **knights / nobles**.

Your turn

4 Work with a partner. Answer the questions.
1. What do you think of the feudal system? Was it fair? Why?/Why not?
2. Can you think of any famous knights from history?
3. Would you like to live in the Middle Ages? Why?/Why not?

THE FEUDAL SYSTEM

In Europe in the Middle Ages – from the 5th to the 15th century – some people owned land and some people lived or worked on the land. This system was called the feudal system. It was a hierarchy because some people were at the top and some people were at the bottom.

1 The ¹................ was at the top of the feudal system. He owned too much land to look after by himself so he divided it up, and gave some of it to people called 'nobles' to rule for him. These different areas of land were called fiefs. When a king died, his son became the owner of the fiefs.

2 The ²................ looked after the king's land. They ruled large fiefs. They paid tax to the king and sometimes helped him in wars and battles. These people were less important than the king in the hierarchy but very important in the local community.

3 Nobles usually employed ³................ to help protect their fiefs. They were often heroes because they were strong and brave, especially in battles. They always helped the king when he asked them and protected him. Most of them were men, but some were women.

4 About 90% of people in the Middle Ages were ⁴................ . They were at the bottom of the hierarchy. They didn't have land or money like the other members of society. They worked on the land for the nobles, growing food and looking after animals. They paid taxes to the nobles and worked all day. Life was very hard for these people.

Find out about one of the first female pilots.

Discovery EDUCATION

2.4 Amelia Earhart, famous flyer

3 CLIL

Art Making a comic

1 Match the comic words with the definitions.

1 plot
2 panel
3 pencilling
4 a sketch
5 layout
6 inking
7 speech bubble
8 lettering

a the position of artwork on a page
b shape containing a character's words
c writing text in a speech bubble
d drawing something in pencil
e drawing something in pen
f a square or rectangular section of a comic
g the story of a comic
h a simple, basic drawing

2 🔊 1.39 Read and listen to the text and check your ideas to Exercise 1.

3 Read the text again. Mark the sentences true (*T*) or false (*F*). Correct the false sentences.

1 A comic usually begins with the artwork.
2 The writer sometimes draws parts of the comic.
3 The artist inks the artwork before pencilling it.
4 Computers usually do lettering.
5 The artist decides the position of speech bubbles.
6 The colourist colours the comic by hand.

Your turn

4 Work with a partner. Design your own comic. Follow the steps in the text.

The Art of Comics

Before an artist starts to draw, a comic generally begins with a 'plot'. The plot is the story of the comic. The comic writer sometimes plans the plot on the page and includes notes, basic sketches and instructions on what happens in each panel or section for the artist to interpret.

When the writer finishes the plot, the artist pencils the story. This is when the artist does a sketch, or a simple basic drawing, of each panel in pencil. During pencilling, the artist decides the layout, position and style of the artwork. After this, the artist then 'inks' the sketches. In this process the artist creates clear, 'line art' in pen. It is still common for the artist to do the pencilling and inking by hand, not on computer.

Next, the artist inserts the dialogue into the speech bubbles. This is called 'lettering'. To do this, the artist usually uses a computer, but they must still plan by hand where the text goes on the page.

Finally, the artist adds colour to the final line art drawings. In the past, the artist did this by hand, but these days they use computers. The artist usually scans hand-drawn inked pages, and sends them to a colourist. The colourist then uses a special computer program to colour the images.

Find out about making a documentary.

Discovery EDUCATION

3.4 Behind the scenes

4 CLIL

Art The Bauhaus movement

1 Look at the photos. Which words in the box can you use to describe each building?

> modern   old-fashioned   practical
> comfortable   functional   attractive   simple

2 🔊 1.40 Read and listen to the text. Which building in Exercise 1 do you think is Bauhaus?

Bauhaus was an art school in Weimar, Germany. German architect Walter Gropius started the school in 1919. The Bauhaus school tried to combine form (the shape of something) and function (how we use something) in architecture so that buildings were practical but also simple. Bauhaus architects didn't like lots of decoration on buildings; they preferred flat roofs, straight lines and geometric shapes. Before Bauhaus, architects used lots of different shapes and colours, and materials like marble, hardwoods and even gold for the decorations in their buildings. Bauhaus used metal, glass, steel or plastic to make their buildings. Typical colours are white, grey and black. The designs for the furniture inside Bauhaus buildings are also simple, and functional.

3 Read the text again. Mark the sentences true *(T)* or false *(F)*. Correct the false sentences.
1. The Bauhaus style began in a school in Germany.
2. Bauhaus buildings are traditional and attractive.
3. The buildings used more basic materials than in the past.
4. You can only see the Bauhaus style in buildings and architecture.

4 🔊 1.41 Listen to the second part of the text about the Bauhaus school and choose the correct answers.
1. The Bauhaus school moved location **twice / three times** before it closed.
2. Former students of the school took their ideas to different parts of **the world / Germany**.
3. A building in an airport in **Chicago / Houston** is an example of Bauhaus architecture.
4. **Josep Lluis Sert / Joan Miró** designed the *Casa Bloc* in Barcelona.

Your turn

5 Work with a partner. Answer the questions.
1. Can you think of any buildings with a similar style to Bauhaus in your town or city?
2. Which buildings do you like in your town or city? What are they made of? What do you like about them?

Find out about the pyramids in Egypt.

Discovery EDUCATION

4.4 The seventh wonder of the world

5 CLIL

ICT Supercomputers

1 Work with a partner. Answer the questions.
1. What do you think the difference is between a personal computer and a supercomputer?
2. What do you think people use supercomputers for?
3. What do the letters CPU mean?

2 🔊 2.38 Read and listen to the text and check your ideas to Exercise 1.

Supercomputers

Personal computers help us to communicate and organise our lives. They help us to work and also to have fun. But in science, the type of computer that we use every day isn't powerful enough. Scientists need more powerful computers to help them understand the world around us. They use these 'supercomputers' to do experiments that might be difficult or dangerous in the real world. Supercomputers are huge and are much faster than personal computers. Some of them can do more than one quadrillion (1,000,000,000,000,000) calculations in a second.

A supercomputer can work so quickly because it has many CPUs. The CPU, or Central Processing Unit is the brain of the computer. It can process information very fast and accurately. Scientists use this power to make virtual physical worlds that help them with research.

Every time you see the weather forecast on TV, you are seeing the work of very powerful supercomputers. Scientists use these computers to tell us if it's going to be sunny at the weekend, to show how aeroplanes can save fuel by flying with the wind, and also how the weather is going to change in the future.

As for the future, experts believe that one day computer scientists will build the ultimate supercomputer that can think and act just like human brains. Perhaps one day computers really will rule the world!

3 Read the text again and answer the questions.
1. What do scientists test with supercomputers?
2. How many operations can a supercomputer do per second?
3. What makes a supercomputer powerful?
4. Why are virtual physical worlds useful to scientists?
5. How can supercomputers help aeroplane pilots?
6. What will the 'ultimate supercomputer' do?

Your turn

4 Work with a partner. How do you think supercomputers can be useful in the following areas?

> health   education   the environment

Find out about two men who look the same.

5.4 Who's real?

6 CLIL

Science Lifecycle of a plastic bag

1 Look at the photos. Which do you think people use to make plastic bags?

wood   metal   oil   water

2 🔊 2.39 Listen to the first part of an interview with an expert on plastic and check your ideas to Exercise 1.

3 🔊 2.39 Listen to the interview again and complete the diagram about making plastic bags.

use   make polyethylene   recycle
extract oil   make plastic bag

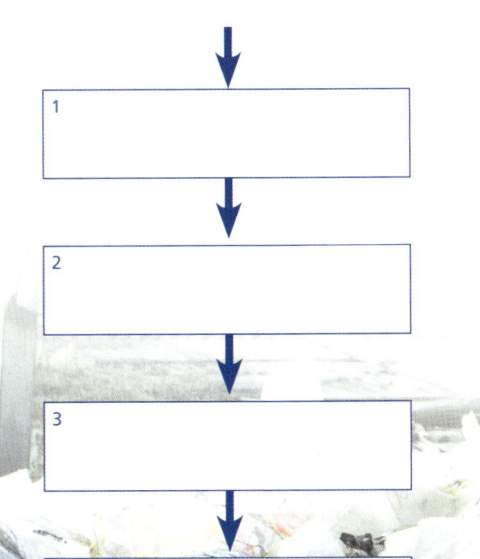

1.
2.
3.
4.
5.

4 🔊 2.40 Listen to the second part of the interview and choose the correct answers.
1 Recycling is part of the **two / three** 'Rs'.
2 We usually use plastic bags **once / twice** before we throw them away.
3 Each year **100,000 / 1 million** marine animals die because of plastic bags.
4 Most plastic bags are **biodegradable / non-biodegradable**.
5 It can take up to **1,000 / 100** years for a plastic bag to decompose.

Your turn

5 Work with a partner. Answer the questions.
1 What alternatives are there to plastic bags?
2 Can you think of any interesting ways to reuse plastic bags?
3 What do you do to help the environment?

Find out about a green building.

6.4 Go green!

7 CLIL

Science Foodborne illness

1 Look at the pictures. What do you know about food poisoning? Have you ever had it?

2 🔊 **2.41** Complete the text with the words in the box. Then listen and check.

> bacteria   symptoms   surface   raw   intestines   spread   headaches   illness

FOODBORNE ILLNESS

Have you ever felt ill after you've eaten something? Yes? Then you've probably had food poisoning. Food poisoning is an ¹.... which you can get when you eat food that contains ².... , viruses or parasites, which enter the stomach and ³.... . This is called a foodborne illness. Common ⁴.... of foodborne illnesses are diarrhoea, vomiting, ⁵.... and fever.

The two most common foodborne illnesses are campylobacter and salmonella. Both of these are bacterial foodborne illnesses and we sometimes find them in ⁶.... (uncooked) meat (especially chicken and turkey), milk, eggs and unclean water.

You can get food poisoning from food which has not been cooked properly or because of 'cross contamination'. This is when bacteria ⁷.... between different foods, surfaces or kitchen equipment. For example, when you prepare raw chicken on a surface and don't clean it before using the same ⁸.... for other food like salad or cooked meat. Another danger is when you keep raw meat above other food in a fridge and liquid from the raw meat falls on to the food below.

3 Read the text again. Mark the sentences true (*T*) or false (*F*). Correct the false sentences.
  1 Bacteria is the only cause of foodborne illness.
  2 Campylobacter and salmonella are viruses.
  3 Uncooked meat can contain campylobacter and salmonella.
  4 Cross contamination is when bacteria pass from one food to another.

4 🔊 **2.42** Listen to a Food Technology teacher and put the four Cs of food safety in the order he talks about them.

> cross-contamination   chilling
> cleaning   cooking

5 🔊 **2.42** Listen again and make notes on the four Cs in Exercise 4.

Your turn

6 Work with a partner. What other ways can you think of for bacteria and infections to spread from person to person?

Find out about loud music.

Discovery EDUCATION

7.4 Medical myths

CLIL

Geography Functional zones

1 Match the photos with the different zones in a city.

industrial zone   residential zone   CBD (central business district)

2 🔊 **2.43** Read and listen to the text and check your ideas to Exercise 1.

FUNCTIONAL ZONES

Functional zones in a city are the areas where people go to do particular things. There are three main functional areas in a modern city: the CBD (central business district), the industrial zone and the residential zone.

The CBD is often called the city centre. It is usually in the historic centre of a city. It has most of the shops and services, like banks, libraries, and also offices and the town hall. There are also places for entertainment like theatres, cinemas and swimming pools. Land is expensive in the CBD so there are often a lot of tall buildings like skyscrapers. Some historic cities don't have these more modern buildings because they want the city to look traditional.

The industrial zone is where the factories, warehouses and industries are. Many years ago, these zones were in the centre of cities, but they moved out, probably because of the noise and pollution. This area is usually less attractive than the central areas. Workers often travel here from where they live, so these zones usually have good transport links for trains and cars to move people, materials and products to and from the factories.

Residential zones are often on the outside of a city. The buildings are newer and the land is cheaper here so this is where people, especially families, live. There are schools and more open spaces like parks, and there is less traffic and pollution than in other zones.

3 Complete the table with the words in the box.

shops   factories   offices   warehouses   parks
swimming pools   skyscrapers   banks   schools

CBD	industrial zone	residential zone

4 Which zone(s) …
1 has got cheaper land?
2 has got more expensive land?
3 has got families?
4 are out of the city centre?
5 is usually a bit ugly?

5 Work with a partner. Can you name the functional zones in your nearest city?

Find out about collecting water.

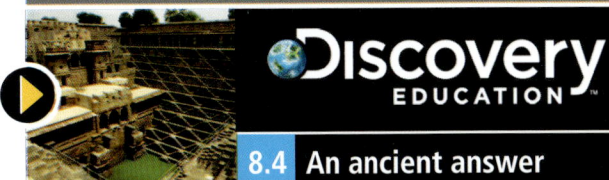

8.4 An ancient answer

Project 1

A sponsored event

SIXFIELDS ANIMAL HOSPITAL
Charity Day
at the Village Hall

Join the fun and help us reach our total of £5,000
Saturday 20th August 1pm

Raffle

food and drink

Sponsored events:
fun run
dance marathon
Hot dog eating contest
music from local band, 'The Singrazers'

Look

1 Look at the poster about the charity day and answer the questions.
   1 What is the charity?
   2 Where is the charity day?
   3 What day is it?
   4 What time does it start?
   5 What sponsored events are there?
   6 What entertainment is there?
   7 How much money do they want to raise?

Prepare

2 Work in groups of three. Plan a charity day in your town and make a poster. Use the questions in Exercise 1 to help you and find photos to put on your poster.

Present

3 Present your poster to the rest of the class. Give extra details about the charity, how friends and family can sponsor you, and the amount of money you want to raise. Which charity day is the class's favourite?

Project 2

A plan of my ideal house

Look

1 Look at the picture of an ideal house and complete the description with the words from the box.

> wardrobe   armchairs   bathrooms
> fridge   kitchen   shelf

My house has got a lot of rooms. Upstairs there are two bedrooms, a games room and two ¹…. . Downstairs there's a living room, a big ²…. , a swimming pool, a gym and a garden. My bedroom has got a massive ³…. for all my clothes, mirrors on all of the walls, a king-sized bed, and two big chests of drawers. In the games room, there's a pool table, a big games centre, with games consoles and a big TV. There's also a ⁴…. full of books, manga comics and computer games. Downstairs the living room is very comfortable with two sofas and four ⁵…. , a coffee table and a cinema-sized TV on the wall. The kitchen's got two microwaves, three dishwashers and a big ⁶…. and freezer for all my food.

Prepare

2 Work in groups of three. Imagine you live together. Design your ideal house and draw a simple plan of it. Think about …
- rooms and what you do in them.
- furniture and what you use it for.
- any other unusual or luxury items.

Present

3 Present your poster to the rest of the class. Which house is the class's favourite?

Project 3

Information leaflet about a festival

MAY DAY

WHERE AND WHEN
May Day is a traditional festival. People celebrate it across Europe and the USA every year on the first day of May. In the UK, it's a public holiday so not many people work on this day.

HISTORY
Most people think that May Day started as a Roman festival to celebrate the end of winter and the start of summer. The first of May used to be the first day of summer in Europe.

ACTIVITIES
In the UK, there are celebrations all around the country to celebrate May Day, with traditional events and activities. One traditional activity is 'May pole dancing'. In this activity, people dance around a tall pole with colourful ribbons. The ribbons create a decorative pattern at the top of the pole as the people dance around it. A lot of schools in rural areas organise maypole dances for their pupils.

Another traditional dance during May Day celebrations is 'morris dancing'. Dancers dress in white clothes with bells attached to them and carry scarves and long wooden sticks. The participants hit their sticks together in the air as they perform a special dance. The bells on their clothes make sounds as they dance to traditional accordion music.

Other traditions include making displays with flowers, decorating houses with flowers and leaves, and special processions through the streets with people dressed in special costumes or fancy dress.

FOOD
There isn't much traditional May Day food, but at May Day events you can typically find traditional British cakes, biscuits and desserts. Fast food like hot dogs and hamburgers are also common.

Look

1 Look at the poster about the festival and complete the information.

name	
location	
date	
history	
activities	
traditional food	

Prepare

2 Work in groups of three. Make a poster about a festival in your country. Use the categories in Exercise 1 to help you, and find photos of the festival to decorate your poster.

Present

3 Present your poster to the rest of the class. Which festival is the class's favourite?

Irregular verbs

infinitive	past simple	past participle
be	was/were	been
become	became	become
begin	began	begun
break	broke	broken
build	built	built
buy	bought	bought
catch	caught	caught
choose	chose	chosen
come	came	come
do	did	done
drink	drank	drunk
drive	drove	driven
eat	ate	eaten
fall	fell	fallen
feed	fed	fed
feel	felt	felt
find	found	found
fly	flew	flown
get	got	got
give	gave	given
go	went	gone
have	had	had
hear	heard	heard
keep	kept	kept
know	knew	known
learn	learnt/learned	learnt/learned
leave	left	left
lose	lost	lost
make	made	made
meet	met	met
pay	paid	paid
put	put	put
read	read	read
run	ran	run
say	said	said
see	saw	seen
send	sent	sent
sit	sat	sat
sleep	slept	slept
speak	spoke	spoken
spend	spent	spent
swim	swam	swum
take	took	taken
teach	taught	taught
tell	told	told
think	thought	thought
wear	wore	worn
win	won	won
write	wrote	written

Phonemic script

consonants

/p/	pencil
/b/	bag
/t/	town
/d/	day
/tʃ/	cheese
/dʒ/	juice
/k/	cake
/g/	get
/f/	food
/v/	very
/θ/	Thursday
/ð/	that
/s/	speak
/z/	zebra
/ʃ/	shoe
/ʒ/	usually
/m/	mum
/n/	name
/ŋ/	sing
/h/	house
/l/	like
/r/	red
/w/	water
/j/	you

vowels

/i:/	see
/ɪ/	sit
/ʊ/	book
/u:/	zoo
/e/	pen
/ə/	teacher
/ɜ:/	bird
/ɔ:/	boring
/æ/	that
/ʌ/	run
/ɑ:/	car
/ɒ/	lost

diphthongs

/eɪ/	say
/ɪə/	hear
/ʊə/	pure
/ɔɪ/	enjoy
/əʊ/	know
/eə/	chair
/aɪ/	buy
/aʊ/	now

Thanks and acknowledgements

The authors and publishers would like to thank all the teachers and consultants who have contributed to the development of this course, in particular:

Argentina: Fernando Armesto; Natalia Bitar; Verónica Borrás; Leonor Corradi; Paz Moltrasio; Diana Ogando; Brazil: Dalmo Carvalho; Roberto Costa; Sônia M. B. Leites; Gloria Paz; Litany Pires Ribeiro; Christina Riego; Renata Condi de Souza; Elizabeth White; Chile: Magdalena Aldunate; M. Cristina Darraidou Diaz; Valentina Donoso; Ana María Páez Jofrré; Ricardo Contreras Marambio; Claudia Ottone; Maria Elena Ramirez; Jacqueline Rondon; Alicia Paez Ubilla; Colombia: Luz Amparo Bautista; Sonia Ruiz Hernández; Sandra Jara; Fabian Jimenez; Bibiana Andrea Piñeros Merizalde; Lucero Amparo Bernal Nieto; Olga Olarte; Bibiana Piñeros; Emelis Rambut; Sonia Ruíz; Poland: Anna Bylicka; Russia: Natalya Melchenkova; Irina Polyakova; Svetlana Suchkova; Irina Vayserberg; Turkey: Ali Bilgin; Angela Çakır; Shirley Nuttal; Cinla Sezgin; Mujgan Yesiloglu

The publishers are grateful to the following for permission to reproduce copyright photographs and material:
Cover: Shutterstock Images/Vibrant Image Studio; Back cover: Alamy/©Marc Hill; p. 7 (BL): Shutterstock Images/Zaretska Olga; p. 8 (B/G): Alamy/©imageimage; p. 9 (a): Alamy/©Peter Wheeler; p. 9 (b): Alamy/©Chloe Johnson; p. 9 (c): Alamy/©Travel Norwich - Chris Ridley; p. 9 (d): Alamy/©Robert Llewellyn; p. 9 (e): Alamy/©Janine Wiedel Photolibrary; p. 9 (f): Alamy/©Tom Merton; p. 9 (g): Alamy/©Gordon Scammell; p. 9 (h): Alamy/©Kumar Sriskandan; p. 9 (i): Alamy/©Iryna Vlasenko; p. 9 (j): Alamy/©David R. Frazier Photolibrary Inc.; p. 10 (TC): Alamy/©Peter Alvey People; p. 10 (a): Alamy/©Kumar Sriskandan; p. 10 (b): Alamy/©Caro; p. 10 (c): Alamy/©D. Hurst; p. 10-11 (d): Getty Images/Richard I'Anson/Lonely Planet Image; p. 12 (TL): Shutterstock Images/indigolotos; p. 12 (TC): Shutterstock Images/Everything; p. 12 (TR): Alamy/©momo_leif; p. 12 (CL): Shutterstock Images/Surrphoto; p. 12 (CR): Shutterstock Images/Feng Yu; p. 12 (BL): Shutterstock Images/anat chant; p. 12 (BR): Shutterstock Images/tale; p. 14 (B/G): Shutterstock Images/Enciktat; p. 14 (TL): Newscom/imago stock&people; p. 15 (CR): Alamy/©Chloe Parker; p. 15 (BC): Comic Relief/©Helen Hasse; p. 15 (BR): Alamy/©David Taylor; p. 16 (CR): Mark Bassett/Cambridge University Press; p. 16 (BL): Shutterstock Images/Chiyacat; p. 16 (BC): Shutterstock Images/sagir; p. 16 (BR): Thinkstock/Paolo_Toffanin/iStock; p. 17 (CL): Alamy/©John Fedele/Blend Images; p. 18 (B/G): Getty Images/Aurora Creative; p. 19 (a): Shutterstock Images/Mavkate; p. 19 (b): Alamy/©AberCPC; p. 19 (c): Shutterstock Images/Chutima Chaochaiya; p. 19 (d): Alamy/©Bill Stormont; p. 19 (e): Alamy/©Jack Sullivan; p. 19 (f): Alamy/©Hybrid Images/Cultura Creative (RF); p. 19 (g): Alamy/©RGB Ventures/SuperStock; p. 19 (h): Shutterstock Images/Diego Cervo; p. 19 (i): Alamy/©Jose Luis Pelaez/Blend Images; p. 19 (j): Alamy/©Steve Smith/Purestock; p. 20 (TL): Alamy/©Archive Images; p. 20 (TR): Alamy/©Rachel Megawhat; p. 21 (TL): Alamy/©Pictorial Press; p. 21 (CR): Alamy/©Photo Researchers; p. 24 (T): Corbis/Government of Chile/Handout; p. 25 (BR): Alamy/©ZUMA Press; p. 25 (C): Getty Images/Pascal Le Segretain; p. 25 (B/G): Alamy/©Ian Dagnall; p. 26 (TL): Alamy/©Liam White; p. 26 (TC): Thinkstock/Jupiterimages/Photos.com; p. 26 (CR): REX; p. 26 (BC): Getty Images /Joe Scarnici/USOC; p. 26 (BR): Alamy/©Keystone Pictures USA; p. 27 (TL): Alamy/©Geraint Lewis; p. 30 (B/G): Shutterstock Images/Jarno Gonzalez Zarraonandia; p. 32 (BR): Rex Feature/John Alex Maguire; p. 36 (TR): Alamy/©Chad Ehlers; p. 36 (B/G): Alamy/©Silvia Groniewicz; p. 37 (B): Shutterstock Images/Alberto Loyo; p. 38 (R): Alamy/©Ron Nickel/Design Pics Inc.; p. 40 (B/G): Thinkstock/flocu/iStock; p. 42 (a): Newscom/CB2/ZOB; p. 42 (b): Alamy/©Thierry GRUN; p. 42-43 (c): Alamy/©Jason Lindsey; p. 43 (CR): Alamy/©Ian Dagnall; p. 44 (TR): Alamy/©Ton Koene; p. 44 (C): Alamy/©brt CIRCUS; p. 44 (CR): Alamy/©Chuck Franklin; p. 44 (a): Alamy/©a-ts; p. 44 (b): Shutterstock Images/omers; p. 44 (c): Shutterstock Images/sue yassin; p. 44 (d): Shutterstock Images/Mile Atanasov; p. 44 (e): Alamy/©Leslie Garland/LGPL; p. 44 (f): Shutterstock Images/ppart; p. 44 (g): Alamy/©Andrii Gorulko; p. 44 (h): Shutterstock Images/Frank Mac; p. 44 (i): Shutterstock Images/ABB Photo; p. 45 (TR): Shutterstock Images/ChameleonsEye; p. 46 (CR): Alamy/©Don Fuchs; p. 46 (B/G): Alamy/©David Foster; p. 47 (B/G): Alamy/©Vicki Beaver; p. 47 (BC): Alamy/©Alaska Stock LLC; p. 48 (CR): Mark Bassett/Cambridge University Press; p. 50 (a): Shutterstock Images/Bonchan; p. 50 (b): Shutterstock Images/VadiCo; p. 50 (c): Shutterstock Images/Elnur; p. 50 (d): Shutterstock Images/Margouillat photo; p. 50 (e): Shutterstock Images/Africa Studio; p. 53 (a): Shutterstock Images/gillmar; p. 53 (b): Shutterstock Images/Alexey Boldin; p. 53 (c): Shutterstock Images/GeorgeMPhotography; p. 53 (d): Shutterstock Images/Sean Nel; p. 53 (e): Shutterstock Images/AG-PHOTO; p. 53 (f): Shutterstock Images/Maksym Dykha; p. 53 (g): Shutterstock Images/Dmitry Melnikov; p. 53 (h): Shutterstock Images/Sergey Peterman; p. 53 (i): Shutterstock Images/RMIKKA; p. 54 (B/G, CR): REX/Bruce Adams; p. 54 (TL): Shutterstock Images/sgm; p. 55 (BL): Alamy/©Pictorial Press; p. 56 (TR): REX/Gavin Roberts/Future Publishing; p. 59 (b): Alamy/©Jochen Schlenker/Robert Harding Picture Library Ltd; p. 59 (TR): Getty Images/Hero Images/Digital Vision; p. 60 (TR): Glow Images/Tetra Images; p. 62 (B/G): Getty Images/Uppercut/Spike Mafford; p. 63 (a): Glow Images/AID/a.collectionRF; p. 63 (b): Alamy/©Terry Vine/Blend Images; p. 63 (c): Alamy/©Angela Hampton/Bubbles Photolibrary; p. 63 (d): Alamy/©Robert Kerr; p. 63 (e): Alamy/©James Brunker; p. 63 (f): Alamy/©philipus; p. 63 (g): Alamy/©aberystwyth; p. 63 (h): Alamy/©Zoonar GmbH/Darya Petrenko; p. 63 (i): Alamy/©Kentaroo Tryman; p. 63 (j): Alamy/©MBI; p. 66 (TR): Superstock/Photononstop; p. 66 (a): Getty Images/Jamie Grill/Photodisc; p. 66 (b): Shutterstock Images/jocic; p. 66 (c): Thinkstock/Michael Dykstra/Hemera; p. 66 (d): Shutterstock Images/Roman Samokhin; p. 66 (e): Shutterstock Images/R. Gino Santa Maria; p. 66 (f): Shutterstock Images/MNI; p. 66 (g): Shutterstock Images/maxim ibragimov; p. 66 (h): Alamy/©Studiomode; p. 67 (BL): Alamy/©Jeff Morgan 04; p. 68 (CL): Shutterstock Images/canadastock; p. 68 (B/G): Alamy/©Anna Omelchenko; p. 68 (C): Shutterstock Images/Hugh Lansdown; p. 69 (T): Alamy/©Linda Schaefer; p. 69 (B): Alamy/©Susan Liebold; p. 69 (C): Alamy/©szefei wong; p. 70 (CL): Agefotostock/Jeff Greenberg; p. 71 (TR): Mark Bassett/Cambridge University Press; p. 72 (CL): Getty Images/Hero Images/Digital Vision; p. 74 (B/G): Alamy/©artpartner.de; p. 76 (TR): Media Ltd/©ncj; p. 76 (BC): Shutterstock Images/Nattika; p. 76 (BL): Shutterstock Images/Krivosheev Vitaly; p. 76 (CR): Shutterstock Images/STILLFX; p. 76 (CL): Shutterstock Images/Dim Dimich; p. 76 (TC): Shutterstock Images/Susan Schmitz; p. 76 (TL): Shutterstock Images/panbazil; p. 77 (C): REX/Isifa Image Service sro; p. 78 (B): Shutterstock Images/jur_ziv; p. 78 (TL): iStock/teekid; p. 78 (TR): Alamy/©Paul Maguire; p. 79 (CR): Alamy/©Flashgun/Cultura Creative (RF); p. 80 (TL): Shutterstock Images/Brberrys; p. 80 (CL): Photo Researchers/FLPA; p. 80 (B/G): Alamy/©RIA Novosti; p. 80 (CR): Alamy/©Robert Pickett/Papilio; p. 81 (B): Shutterstock Images/Matt Gibson; p. 82 (CR): Alamy/©Chris Rout; p. 82 (BR): Alamy/©Monty Rakusen/Cultura Creative; p. 82 (CL): Getty images/kali9; p. 83 (TR): Thinkstock/BananaStock; p. 84 (B/G): Alamy/©David Wall; p. 85 (a): Alamy/©Matelly/Cultura RM; p. 85 (b): Alamy/©Odilon Dimier/PhotoAlto; p. 85 (c): Alamy/©Denise Hager/Catchlight Visual Services; p. 85 (d): Alamy/©Sally and Richard Greenhill; p. 85 (e): Alamy/©Image Source; p. 85 (f): Alamy/©Tim Hall/Cultura Creative; p. 85 (g): Alamy/©Tim Hall/Cultura Creative; p. 85 (h): Alamy/©Mai Chen; p. 85 (i): Alamy/©keith morris; p. 85 (j): Alamy/©Mikhail Lavrenov; p. 86 (TC): AgeFotostock/YURI ARCURS; p. 86 (TR): Alamy/©HermesMereghetti; p. 86 (BL): Alamy/©TravelStockCollection - Homer Sykes; p. 88 (TR): Alamy/©ZUMA Press Inc; p. 88 (TC): Alamy/©LHB Photo; p. 88 (TL): Alamy/©Bill Bachman; p. 90 (CR): Shutterstock Images/foodfoto; p. 90 (T): Shutterstock Images/Romiana Lee; p. 92 (C): Alamy/©David Grossman; p. 92 (CR): Getty Images/MCT; p. 92 (BC): REX/Andrew Price; p. 92 (BR): Alamy/©Manfred Grebler; p. 93 (TR): Alamy/©Moxie Productions/Blend Images; p. 109 (TR): Alamy/©Blend Images; p. 109 (TC): Alamy/©Bill Stormont; p. 113 (TR): Alamy/©MBI; p. 113 (TC): Thinkstock/Michael Dykstra/Hemera; p. 115 (TR): Alamy/©Cultura Creative (RF); Alamy/©Bill Stormont; p. 119 (a): Shutterstock Images/Claudio Divizia; p. 119 (b): Alamy/©AlanWrigley; p. 119 (CL): REX/Tony Kyriacou; p. 120 (TR): Alamy/©Everett Collection Historical; p. 121 (TL): Thinkstock/Zoonar RF; p. 121 (TCL): Shutterstock Images/Barbro Bergfeldt; p. 121 (TCR): Alamy/ ©Spectral; p. 121 (TR): Thinkstock/TongRo Images; p. 121 (B): Thinkstock/defun/iStock; p. 122 (TR): Alamy/©Pete Titmuss; p. 122 (CL): Shutterstock Images/ Viktor1; p. 122 (C): Alamy/©Cultura RM; p. 123 (1): Shutterstock Images/Ivan Pavlov; p. 123 (2): Alamy/©eye35.pix; p. 123 (3): Alamy/©Topsy; p. 126 (TL): Alamy/©International Photobank; p. 126 (TR): Alamy/©Jack Sullivan; p. 126 (CR): Alamy/©Paul Gapper.

The publishers are grateful to the following illustrators:
Janet Allinger p. 13, 56, 61, 112; David Belmonte (Beehive Illustration): p. 12, 75, 78, 94, 114; Anni Betts p. 6, 34 (T), 58 (C), 87 (R), 116; Galia Bernstein (NB Illustration): p. 32, 88, 108, 115; Seb Camagajevac p. 117; Russ Cook p. 28 (B), 34 (B), 110 (TR); A Corazon p. 116; Nigel Dobbyn (Beehive Illustration): p. 4, 31, 39, 56, 57, 70, 91 (BR), 110 (TC), 112, 118; Mark Duffin p. 28 (T), 41, 60, 125; emc p. 5; Bob Lea p. 52; Q2A Media Services, Inc. p. 10, 14, 15, 22, 24, 25, 36, 37, 46, 47, 49, 58 (TR), 59, 64, 68, 69, 80, 81, 87 (L), 90, 91 (CR), 111; Sean Tiffany p. 22, 49, 64, 87 (L).

All video stills by kind permission of:
Discovery Communications, LLC 2015: p. 8 (1, 2, 4), 11, 14, 18 (1, 2, 4), 21, 24, 30 (1, 2, 4), 33, 36, 40 (1, 2, 4), 43, 46, 52 (1, 2, 4), 55, 58, 62 (1, 2, 4), 65, 68, 74 (1, 2, 4), 77, 80, 84 (1, 2, 4), 87, 90, 116, 117, 118, 119, 190, 121, 122, 123;
Cambridge University Press: p. 8 (3), 16, 18 (3), 26, 30 (3), 38, 40 (3), 48, 52 (3), 60, 62 (3), 70, 74 (3), 82, 82 (3), 92.

The publishers are grateful to the following contributors:
Blooberry and emc design limited: concept design
emc design limited: text design and layouts
QBS Learning: cover design and photo selection
Ian Harker and dsound: audio recordings
Integra Software Services Pvt. Ltd.: video production
Nick Bruckman and People's TV: voxpop video production
Hart McCleod: video voiceovers
Anna Whitcher: video management
Jeremy Bowell: editorial services
Getty Images: music